THE EDGE

MICHAEL HEPPELL

Bestselling author of *Flip It*

HODDER &
STOUGHTON

First published in Great Britain in 2012 by Hodder & Stoughton
An Hachette UK company

1

Copyright © Michael Heppell 2012

A CIP catalogue record for this title is available from the British Library

ISBN 978 1 444 74148 3
Ebook ISBN 978 1 444 74063 9

Typeset in Celeste by Palimpsest Book Production Limited,
Falkirk, Stirlingshire

Printed and bound by Clays Ltd, St Ives plc

Hodder & Stoughton policy is to use papers that are natural,
renewable and recyclable products and made from wood grown in
sustainable forests. The logging and manufacturing processes are
expected to conform to the environmental regulations of the
country of origin.

Hodder & Stoughton Ltd
338 Euston Road
London NW1 3BH

www.hodder.co.uk

THE EDGE

For Emma

Contents

Introduction

You've made it! Your life's perfect and you're so successful at everything you do that it hurts.

No?

I'm guessing that's why you've picked up this book. You're dissatisfied. You know there's more and you'd like some of it. And why not? When you look at highly successful people you don't get jealous, you take a moment to consider how they did it. You want to know what it is that makes them special. What gives them the Edge?

Success leaves tracks, and they become more visible the more you look for them. The more you ask questions, the more you probe and the deeper you go, the more you realise that there is no magic bullet. But you will find formulas, ideas and strategies that you can learn, master and then apply in your own life. And you can do it right now.

This book is packed with those ideas and they will work – if you test them. Reading the book may inspire you but it's doing what I share that will define you. Most of the ideas you'll read about come from years of studying people who have what I'm referring to in this book as the Edge. You can label the Edge as many things; success, achievement, brilliance, genius, talent. They all work.

DEFINING YOUR OWN EDGE

I don't know which of the ideas here will work best for you but I do know many of them will have a dramatic effect on your ability to find and define your own Edge. You'll read about lots of super successful people from business, sport, the military, TV and a host of other disciplines. My goal isn't for you to become just like them; you can't. No one ever emulated someone just by reading a book about them. I want you to find your own Edge, to discover what it is that makes you brilliant and then use these pages as the inspiration to go for it.

THE INTERVIEWS

Writing about people who have the Edge is of course very subjective. Your idea of someone who has the Edge may be completely different from mine. When I started this project I decided to interview as many people with the Edge as possible. During the interviews one of the questions I often asked was, 'Who do you believe has the Edge?' And if my interviewee personally knew the person they named then I'd ask for an introduction to further my research. Some very interesting names came up; people who you may or may not consider to have the Edge.

Does Sir Richard Branson have the Edge? I think so but perhaps you don't. You may be more a fan of sports personalities than of champions in business. That's great. In fact I encourage you to find the examples you agree with and aspire to be more like them. But be careful not to read this book with blinkers on. Humility was one key characteristic of most people with the Edge and a constant search for knowledge was another. Keeping one eye on the future while being in the present was identified as a key skill. Even some of the smaller things like taking notes and following things through were seen as classic attributes.

Edge-It

My profile of someone with the Edge will be different from yours.

Many of the ideas that were shared were practised by almost everyone I interviewed. Should I say who they are and share their opinions? When I asked my interviewees if they would mind being cited alongside particular ideas or thoughts, almost all said they would rather not be quoted and some asked not to be named at all. It wasn't because they didn't stand by what they had said: it was because they didn't want people to think that they professed to have the Edge.

THE RESEARCH

My research isn't scientific. I didn't partner with a university or have a team of people carry out multiple diagnostics on thousands of participants. I carried out thirty-seven formal interviews and I've informally interviewed hundreds of amazing people while working in personal development for the last eighteen years. I did read a bunch of research papers and occasionally posted a quick question on Facebook or Twitter, then took inspiration from the responses.

Many of the examples come from my own life experiences. I don't claim to have the Edge but I have had lots of things happen in my life that range from tragic to fantastic. Some of those experiences and what I learned from them had to be included in this book. They were defining moments for me. The big stuff and the unforgettable, such as remembering the moment I discovered what living by your values really means, or how I felt when, with my class, I watched our teacher jump out of a window because he thought the school was about to blow up.

Towards the end of the project I gave the whole book to two members of my team and asked them to throw in their ideas. It's the first time I've done that and I'm delighted to say the results were brilliant. Throughout the whole process my brilliant wife, business and writing partner Christine came up with dozens of examples, insights, thoughts, corrections (plenty of them) and generally contributed with content. So when I say 'I', think 'we'.

WHY IT'S LIKE A BABY CROCODILE

In the past I've been criticised for making concepts too compli-cated or too easy. 'Too much detail.' 'Not enough depth.' So let's just say from the off that though I am writing this book for you I don't know you. I don't know how much depth or detail you want so I've written it in a way that will give you lots of infor-mation but in short bursts rather than pages and pages of detail. The reason for this is that I've made an assumption. The assumption is that you don't have a lot of time. I want to respect that, so I'll do my very best not to repeat the same point or illustrate an idea with a further six stories that only slightly differ from the last. If you want to find out more, you'll find out more, and that's why I've made it short and snappy.

KNOWING WHAT YOU KNOW VS DOING WHAT YOU KNOW

I also know that you want to find your Edge quickly and that one of your overriding passions is to make your life better. Some of the ideas here, then, are very simple. In fact you may read them and wonder how they'll help you to find your Edge when you already knew that! Here's the thing: for every ten people who read *The Edge* there will be ten different opinions of what's basic, advanced, easy or hard. So when you do find one of those sections where you already know it (and you will), take a step back to check in on how well you're performing in that area right now.

One of the key characteristics of people with the Edge is this: they are open to new ideas and concepts first – they'll do the detail later. So will we. I've created this book to focus on the key areas of finding the Edge. I'm sure I've missed some and I'm sure some will interest you more than others. That's why this book is designed for you to jump in and out of the content. You can just read the chapters which interest you most (if you're picky), read the ones you need right now (if you're in a hurry) or read everything from cover to cover (the preferred option of the non-picky reader with a little more time).

EDGERS

Early in the writing process I found myself getting frustrated with having to write 'those who have the Edge' each time I wanted to describe a person who had the Edge. Through various brainstorms we came up with the name 'Edger' to describe a person who has the Edge. It's not perfect and if you can think of a better name then please let me know. I have to go with something, so Edger it is. If you like it, great, you'll see it a lot. If not, I'm sure it'll grow on you.

As you read this book you'll repeatedly see this Edge-It symbol.

It indicates what I've called 'Edge-Its': sound bites of information that go with the piece you're reading. Some are there to focus key points, others to make you question what you're reading. Some are there just to break the page up. I wouldn't advise you read the whole book just using the Edge-Its but if you want the essence of a chapter then you'll get it from the Edge-Its fairly quickly.

Finally, and I've put this in every book I've written, I'm afraid that just reading the book isn't enough. You've got to test the ideas, question the concepts and practise the principles. One of the first people I interviewed during the research phase challenged me on precisely this point, saying, 'Do you really think people can just read a book and get the Edge?'

'No I don't,' I replied, 'but I do passionately believe that with your insight and the help of others there will be enough in my book for the reader to feel inspired by what they read. Then, when they test the ideas, they will find improvements in every area of life where they choose to apply them. It's only by encouraging readers to take action that we will help them to find their Edge.'

'I like it,' he said.

The secret isn't in the knowing – it's in the doing! So let's begin.

1

Instinct, Intuition and Insight

I

t's 11 p.m. and you're heading back to your hotel. It really has been one of those days and the prospect of walking through reception, heading straight to your room, flicking on the TV and climbing into your nice warm bed has spurred you on for the last half-mile or so.

You didn't plan to be out so late; a combination of circumstances, including a last-minute decision to grab a pizza, a glass of something with the new team you have been working with today, was the final piece of the jigsaw which means you're arriving back at the hotel five hours later than planned.

You walked this route this morning. You didn't choose the hotel; your office has a logistics department which makes sure they get the best deal at any hotel they can find within a two-mile radius of the city office. It's clean and reasonably comfortable and you know you'll sleep well as you've been up for hours.

As you walk you suddenly feel a slight pang of anxiety. There's no logical reason for this feeling. The road is well lit and cars pass every couple of minutes. You can't quite place it but you know something isn't quite right. You look over your shoulder expecting to see someone. There's nobody there but you do see a black cab coming towards you. Its light is on. You could stop it, hop in and be at your hotel in a few minutes.

Should you hail it? It's only another quarter of a mile to the hotel. You can walk that in five minutes. What will the driver think? Your anxiety builds. If you do want the cab you'll need to stop it quickly; you have two seconds to decide.

What would you do?

After reading the last few paragraphs, most people would say I'd stop that cab and dive straight into it. But would you? Really? Or might the embarrassment of telling the driver the name of your hotel, then him pointing out that it's 'just around that corner', be too much?

A few years ago I ran a leadership programme for the Metropolitan Police's High Performance Officers scheme. There were some very bright men and women on that programme from all ranks and parts of the force. Over lunch one day I was talking to one officer about personal safety. We discussed knife crime, muggings, gang fights and a whole bunch of other subjects which, on reflection, weren't best suited to the lunch table. He passionately believed that learning self-defence in the traditional sense was useless. 'The idea that you could take a few classes and think you'll remember what you've learned in the middle of an attack is farcical. We shouldn't be teaching self-defence, we should be teaching self-preservation.'

I asked him to explain what he meant by 'self-preservation' and this was his explanation. 'You know when you're walking down a street and suddenly you get that feeling that you shouldn't be there? Well, you're right: you shouldn't.'

Edge-It

When you get that feeling that something's wrong and you shouldn't be there. Well, you're right: **it is and you shouldn't.**

He believed that if this simple explanation was taught to young people and reaffirmed later in life then there would be a significant reduction in the amount of unprovoked attacks in the Metropolitan Police area.

What do you think?

Those with the Edge know how to listen to and act on their intuition. It often screams, sometimes whispers, but it's always there, keeping them safe and helping them to make the right decisions.

The Edge

Edgers use their intuition live. By this I mean they are constantly making decisions using their intuition rather than having the 'aha' moment where they recalled their intuitive instinct but perhaps didn't act on it.

Edge-It
Listen to and act on your intuition.

Intuition comes from the Latin word 'intueri' meaning 'to look inside' or 'to contemplate'. I love the simplicity of that. And there are scales of intuition, from common sense to insight. The more often you use your intuition (even forcing yourself to do so) the easier it becomes to act on it. Highly intuitive people have fewer instances where they say 'I knew that' (past tense) and more where they just know it (in the now). You could look at it like this:

Intuition Grid

High Frequency	
Habitual Methodical **Ability to translate data quickly** Has ways of working that work	**Totally intuitive** Acts on impulse **Feels confident** Future based **Never looks back**
Needs data Constant information required for decision making **Doesn't stretch their intuitive reasoning**	**Occasionally has 'aha!' moments** Recognises they have used intuition after the event **Wishes they 'listened' to their intuition more often**
Low Frequency	

Common Sense ⟶ Insight

The Intuition Grid is a simple way to explore the way you use your intuition. Let's take a look at the four quadrants:

- Common Sense – Low Frequency. This person wouldn't be described as very intuitive. On the rare occasions when they have to make a decision they need data, and plenty of it. They can often be heard saying, 'I don't know.'
- Common Sense – High Frequency. This person eats up data and can take in vast amounts of knowledge. They're the ones who'll have finished reading a spreadsheet while you're still working out the headings.
- Insight – Low Frequency. These people have their moments of genius and when they do have an 'aha' moment they are pleasantly surprised to discover how right they were. Unfortunately 'were' is the key word here. They know they have insight but, because they rarely use it, they tend not to act on it as often as they should.
- Insight – High Frequency. These people are constantly using their intuition and making decisions based on feelings. They have an uncanny knack of being able to visualise future events and outcomes and act on their gut instinct. Many Edgers fall into this quadrant.

The more you explore intuition the more you realise it's linked to every part of your life. For example:

- Health: I knew I shouldn't have eaten that last slice.
- Relationships: I think we need to talk.
- Finding relationships: It was an instant attraction.
- Business: I knew we should have changed our supplier.
- Parenting: OK, what is it?
- Friendships: There was just something odd about him.
- Money: It felt too good to be true – and it was!
- Career: I should have gone for that job. I'd have got it.
- Safety: Hail the cab.

Edge-It

Edgers develop their intuition and use it like an emotional radar.

What I mean here by emotional radar is that Edgers are constantly scanning their environment, those connected to them and the data they have. I had lunch the other day with a guy who spent seven years training the Special Forces to be special. I'd tell you who he was but then I (or probably he) would have to kill you. He taught the very best how to be better.

Some of his ideas made absolute common sense. I'd like to think I would automatically apply them in a survival situation. Others were much more subtle, such as tuning into smells and how to know when it's actually best to get rid of your weapon. What was most interesting was his belief that intuition can be learned. He would drill into soldiers, 'What are you feeling during an exercise?' 'Why didn't it feel right?' Sometimes they knew exactly why, other times they couldn't put their finger on it, but it felt as real as pages of data. On one field exercise he would encourage soldiers to predict when they would be infiltrated by an outside group. Some were able to do this well but didn't know how they did it. On closer examination it came down to sound and smell. After three days in the field the smell of a clean person can travel for miles. Alterations in birdsong and the slightest ambient change can be felt. Being able to identify, tap into and fine tune these signs helps Special Forces to develop their intuitive nature to the next level.

One of the most famous examples of intuition occurred in the 1950 Monaco Grand Prix. A massive accident had occurred but it was hidden around a bend. Before the marshals had a chance to stop the race two other cars had ploughed into it. Racing legend and undoubted Edger Juan Manuel Fangio rounded the bend next, but something caused him to slow down. This split-second decision enabled him to avoid the crash and go on to win the race. Fangio was one of the greatest drivers of all time, winning five world championships and still holds the highest percentage of wins in Formula One. When he was asked why and how he knew he needed to reduce his speed he put it down to intuition. In Fangio's case, this was based on his years of experience combined with a brilliant brain which was able to decipher minute details that other drivers would have seen but failed to interpret.

As he approached the corner he noticed there was something different in the crowd of spectators. Instead of seeing thousands of blurred faces he noticed darkness where the pink of faces should have been. His deep intuition instantly registered that the crowd weren't looking at him but at what was ahead of him, and he instinctively knew that this meant they must be looking at something serious, so he slowed down. He reacted in a fraction of a second, travelling at well over 100 mph while racing on one of the most difficult circuits in the world. Incredible.

Perhaps the most exciting part of your intuition is how naturally brilliant it is to start with. A simple study carried out by University College London discovered that, in certain circumstances, by removing the opportunity to analyse a situation for too long and thus making it necessary to go straight to using intuition you are more likely to make a better decision.

Edge-It
You'll make **better decisions** using your intuition than trying to analyse **under pressure**.

The researchers demonstrated this by presenting subjects with 650 identical symbols on a screen. Amongst them they would place a single odd symbol. When each set of symbols flashed onto the screen the subject was asked to find the odd one and indicate if it was on the left- or right-hand side of the screen. Eye-tracking software followed the subject's eye movement. The length of time the images were shown was increased and decreased.

Amazingly, researchers discovered a higher accuracy rate when subjects were given 'no scrutinising time' – i.e. a fraction of a second when their intuition took over – compared to when they were given over one second and felt they had time to consider.

Edgers have brilliant intuition because they listen to it, feed it and question it every day. They trust their instinct and know that invariably it is correct. The more often they use it, the more finely tuned their intuition becomes. The more finely tuned your intuition is, the easier it is to make instinctive incisive decisions. The most important part of this virtuous circle is in its beginning.

2

The Edger's Cycle

The more you study those with the Edge the more you notice a constant cycle which drives them to ever-greater things. I believe it looks like this.

Success

Dissatisfaction

Solution

Action

It really doesn't matter where this cycle starts but often it starts with being dissatisfied.

DISSATISFACTION

Edgers are dissatisfied, believing there has to be a better way. James Dyson invented the cylinder vacuum cleaner because he was dissatisfied with the poor suction from traditional bag-based machines. Charles Kettering was motivated to create the starter motor because so many people were being injured (and even killed) using a crankshaft to start a car.

Edge-It
Edgers are notoriously dissatisfied.

And it goes beyond physical invention. The desire to improve ways of working, administrative tasks, quality of life, justice, the internet and the law have all come from a dissatisfaction with the 'old' way of doing things.

SOLUTION

Being dissatisfied is a common trait. We all feel dissatisfied at one time or another. What begins to set the Edger apart is their desire to find a solution. Their solution-based thinking takes many forms. Some are fervent note-takers, others ask questions, most probe deeply into the situation for a greater understanding.

When the creative mind takes over, the solution becomes apparent. It's rarely perfect, usually it's just the outline of an idea, but the Edger knows that thinking about a solution is never enough. There's no right or wrong time, but once they feel they have a solution they are driven to take action.

Edge-It

When the creative mind takes over, the solution becomes apparent.

ACTION

The actions come quickly. Inventors will fashion a version of their idea from anything they can find. Drawers are ransacked, utensils are commandeered and Gaffa (duct/duck) tape is seized while the budding inventor creates their prototype. It's the same with web development. Waiting until the idea is fully formed is a misnomer for a web entrepreneur. Get something online and start testing it – live, now.

These actions can often create a series of problems of their own. Especially as Edgers could be better at sharing what it is they are trying to achieve. Those close to them report seeing chaos reign as they desperately attempt to get what's in their head into some kind of working model. Their frustration can boil over, as was frequently the case with Steve Jobs while creating Apple products. It must have been very frustrating for Jobs when he knew exactly how he wanted something to be but could not always articulate it. On countless occasions he would scream at software and hardware developers, as they came to him with their version of his vision, 'Why don't you get it?'

It is of course taking action that really sets the Edger apart. I wish I had a pound for everyone who has shared with me his or her next big idea but didn't do anything with it. I've met the person who claims it was really him who came up with the world wide web and met also the 'true inventor' of satnav. I bet you've met a few of these 'great thinkers' too – the one's who had the great idea but just couldn't execute it.

Edge-It

It's taking action that really sets the Edger apart.

SUCCESS

For the few who become dissatisfied, find a solution, take action and have it all come together the reward is success. But for the Edger it is rarely about the success. In fact for many people with the Edge, success is a distraction. As they experience success, their lives and businesses change and, with change, new problems become visible. They can't ignore the issues; they're real, something needs to be done and once again they are dissatisfied.

This cycle can be seen in many areas of life:

In sports
A successful natural athlete wins everything at a low level.
She becomes dissatisfied and needs a new challenge.
She needs to compete at a higher level but to do this she needs to train.
She takes action, trains hard and finds the right people to support her.
Success!
She starts winning everything . . .

In politics
A local person sees what's wrong.
They campaign for change.
They believe the best way to make a difference is to be elected.
They run a campaign and win the power to influence change.
They actively influence change – but they want to do more.

In business
The entrepreneur sees a 'gap'.
They work out what needs to change.
They test solutions and get some buy-in.
They take it to the next level.
They enjoy some success.
It's good but there has to be a better way – right?

In relationships

You want a partner.

You realise you're not going to find them sitting in front of the TV.

You get out and about and meet people.

You find someone.

You take action to make the sparks fly and the romance blossoms.

They commit to you, you commit to them.

You're in a relationship!

You realise the relationship won't thrive if you just sit together in front of the TV.

Edgers are aware of this cycle and believe that the faster it spins the better. They constantly want to reinvent and reinvigorate their lives, because they really do believe there's always a better way.

HOW TO GET THE BEST OUT OF EACH PHASE OF THE EDGE CYCLE

Dissatisfied

Don't you just hate it when people are dissatisfied but they: (a) don't know why, or (b) do know why but aren't prepared to do anything about it?

When you find yourself feeling dissatisfied take a moment to consider where the solution lies. Is it inside or outside your circle of influence? If it's outside and you feel there is nothing you can do then perhaps it's time to change your focus and busy your mind with something that you can change, even if it's just a small part of the overall problem or another challenge you face. If it's inside your circle of influence then get to work and find a way to change how you're feeling. This is all about taking action.

Edge-It

When you find yourself feeling dissatisfied, quickly work out if a solution is either within or outside your circle of influence.

Solution

Some people are lucky. Their brains are wired in such a way that they find themselves constantly thinking of new ideas and better ways to do things. Others need a jolt. One of the most effective ways to work through the above problem is to use a few well-placed questions such as:

Have I experienced something similar to this problem before?

How can I change a part of it?

What would [fill in a thinker you admire] do?

Who else can help me with this?

Why did I just think of them?

Where can I get knowledge on this?

What's a small variation I could try?

What's a major modification I could make?

The Edge

Many Edgers find thinking on paper a great way to tackle their problems. Mind Maps, graphs, quadrants, sketches, doodles and lists all get the brain thinking differently.

Take photographs and videos of things that inspire you. Find out how stuff works and set aside a bit of time to review your results. Mix it up. Put yourself in some new situations. Meet some people from outside of your sector or social group. Visit a new country, town or city.

Edge-It

Think about it like this: the best idea to solve the most common problem probably hasn't been thought of yet. You could hold the key to that solution.

Action

Having brilliant ideas means nothing unless you're prepared to take some action. Often the magnitude of the challenge stops people from taking action, but not the Edger. It doesn't matter what they do so long as they do something to kick-start the process. Facebook didn't start as Facebook; Mark Zuckerberg used the basic concepts of the site in other formats first. And the mobile phone you use today is unrecognisable compared to the bricks we carried in the 1990s.

By taking action you breathe life into an idea. The old doctrine of ready, aim, fire has been replaced by fire, fire, fire!

You're far better off taking action – adjusting; taking action – assessing; taking action and adjusting, rather than just planning, planning, planning.

One of the most impressive things I noticed about Edgers was their speed when it comes to taking action. They call rather than email. They ask for decisions now. They make a commitment and go for it. They shrink timescales. They'll adjust on the fly. They do it fast. They do it now.

Edge-It

Edgers don't email. They pick up the phone and make a call.

Success

It worked! You've turned your dissatisfaction into success. Here's where the advice changes a little. While the other sections of this book are all about what to do next, this is the time to stop and take stock of what you've achieved up to this point. Think about what you've accomplished in your lifetime. Give yourself a moment to enjoy what you've done. As an Edger it won't be too long before you'll find something else to be dissatisfied about, but for now you've got to the top. Take a moment to enjoy the view.

The Result: Confidence

This success cycle also creates huge amounts of confidence for you. As you would imagine, confidence and having the Edge go hand in hand. But you have to take the right actions to become confident. Simply demanding more confidence from yourself won't work. This is where the Edge cycle builds your self-confidence brilliantly. Let's take each part and break it down.

DISSATISFACTION

Being dissatisfied is where some people live their entire lives. They know there must be something better, but in order to tap into 'better' they also know they'll have to change to achieve it. And as that something usually starts with them taking a step outside of the famous comfort zone and involves risk and hard work, many are put off. Here's my tip: start getting out of your comfort zone with the small things first. Have a conversation with a stranger, do something a little unusual, try a food that is outside of your normal eating habits. The more you do this with the smaller stuff the more you'll feel able to do it with some of the slightly bigger stuff. Soon you'll find that being dissatisfied doesn't need to mean being stagnant and you'll tackle your frustrations head-on to find a . . .

SOLUTION

Now, because you are no longer disengaged, your brilliant brain will start to think of solutions. The momentum that comes from doing this and the excitement of feeling that you can make a difference to literally anything will start to spur you on. You've realised that you can do something about this feeling of dissatisfaction, you're brimming with ideas and your confidence is building, so now it's time to take . . .

ACTION

As always the secret is in the doing. Reading this chapter is a great start but it's the testing of the concepts that makes the difference. Yes, I know I'm beginning to sound like a stuck record/CD/MP3 (delete according to age) but it really is the actions you'll take that will define you and, more specifically, your level of confidence.

Edge-It

Just thinking about being more confident will never be enough. You have to prove to yourself that you are committed and that means taking action.

Yes, you can start to build your confidence by thinking positive thoughts about being confident, but nothing will give you more of a boost than getting stuck in and taking action. Here are a few simple actions you can take to get you started.

- Pick up the phone and talk rather than hiding behind email.
- Challenge your boss – be careful.
- Ask for help – people want to help you.
- If you make a mistake, own up – it's liberating.

- Go and see someone who needs a visit; that's a visit, not a text.
- Speak up in a meeting – leaving the room afterwards and 'wishing you'd said' isn't enough.
- Make a public commitment – what are you going to do?
- Ask someone out – obviously this one is for the singles.
- Have a conversation with a stranger – on the bus, at the supermarket, in the pub (this could link well with the one above).
- If something's not right, complain – but do it nicely.
- Host a dinner party – it WILL be a success.

The more action you take the more impact you'll have, the more impact you have the more you'll accomplish, and that leads to . . .

SUCCESS

Yup, nothing feels as good as success, but please beware, because just a few steps on from being successful and confident is being successful and arrogant. Don't worry, that won't happen to you because you'll read what real Edgers do to be successful and confident without being arrogant in the following pages.

The confidence that comes with success is wonderful because it's usually been earned. But don't expect it to last for ever, because just as your confidence is growing, so is your comfort zone; and with a bigger comfort zone you'll have the desire for even more confidence and sooner or later that will create dissatisfaction.

And so the cycle continues.

3

Habits

Daily habits, by their very nature, tend to go unnoticed by the person who carries them out. For most it's just what they do. However, these habits fashion the foundations that those with the Edge build on. The stronger the foundations the higher the tower. Creating new habits (or getting rid of old bad ones) takes much more effort than maintaining the ones you already have. So it's worth investing a bit of time and energy designing and creating a new set of habits that will become part of your daily life and help you to become the person you want to be.

Edge-It

It's time and energy well spent, considering and designing a new set of habits to help you to become the person you ultimately want to be.

Those with the Edge have many comparable habits. Some are extreme: ice-cold showers, obsessional time-keeping or daily chanting. Others are more conventional: daily prayer, maintaining regular eating habits, a catch-up telephone call to Mum. From the dozens we identified, here are twenty of the most common habits of those with the Edge:

1. **They wake up early.** In the vast majority of cases those with the Edge wake up early. The exact time varies depending on their work; for

people involved with the arts or music, for example, rising at 9.00 a.m. could be considered early whereas for those in the military, getting up at 7.00 a.m. is deemed a long lie-in.

2. **They wake up, then get up.** Edgers tend not to stay in bed for long once they've woken up. Their systems are almost programmed so that once they are awake they get out of bed and get moving.

3. **They eat well.** Getting the best-quality nutrition is essential. Quality fuel feeds the body and brain, so eating is an important part of the day, and Edgers enjoy their food. They are conscious of what they eat and consider food to be fuel. They often spend a disproportionate amount of time choosing the right foods to ensure that when they do eat it's nutritional and also extremely enjoyable.

4. **They hydrate.** They stay hydrated, making sure they avoid feeling thirsty. Most start their day with at least 500 ml of water, knowing that feeling thirsty is a sign of being severely dehydrated and is something to be avoided.

5. **They stay fit.** Exercise is scheduled into their routine, with most doing a minimum of four exercise sessions every week. Many exercise every day; even if it's just a quick run or twenty minutes stretching, it's a vital habit.

6. **They watch the news – but only once a day.** Almost everyone we interviewed watched the news, but only once. Very few watched local news channels.

7. **They read quality newspapers and 'speed browse' others.** Because those with the Edge can take in a lot of information they are able to read a newspaper in a fraction of the time it takes most others. Almost all read at least one newspaper a day.

8. **They listen.** The ability to listen first is a powerful habit amongst the Edgers. Even if they are asked their opinion they normally turn the question around and ask others what they think first.

9. **They have clean shoes.** A funny one but nonetheless an important one. This is more than taking care of personal appearance. Edgers look after their shoes. They keep them clean, put them away neatly, use shoe-trees and pride themselves on shiny well-presented footwear.

10. **They keep their phone charged.** You'll never hear an Edger come out with the dismal excuse of 'my phone ran out of power', because they maintain the vital habit of keeping it fully charged.

11. **They put things away.** I wish this weren't true, as I could be better at this one, but it is. Edgers tend to be tidy and very good at putting things away after they've used them. The obvious benefit being that you don't waste time looking for anything because you always know where things are.

12. **They schedule the 'stuff'.** Haircuts, massages, meetings, dental appointments, etc. are all scheduled well in advance. My own hairdresser shared this one with me when he revealed that all of his

most successful clients book their next appointment before they leave his salon. Now this could be a pitch to get people to book more appointments but he swears it's true.

13. **They write things down.** Keeping a notepad and pencil handy is an essential habit of Edgers. Jonathan Raggett, a leading hotelier with global responsibility for a range of luxury hotels, has a brilliant memory but he carries a small pocket-sized Moleskin notebook in which he constantly records thoughts and ideas for improvements. It's not that he doesn't trust his memory or that he doesn't use electronic devices. His notes are the firm basis for his actions.

14. **They keep records**. Receipts, who agreed to what, minutes of meetings, verbal agreements, timescales – important details where it's better to have a record of the event rather than a vague memory or an opinion.

15. **They love precision.** If it's important to them they'll want it to be just right. They'll spend a disproportionate amount of time making sure it is.

16. **They service rather than fix.** Prevention is better than cure. It's also more cost effective and saves valuable time. From cars to central heating systems, they make sure their technical equipment is working at its peak. Regular servicing means things don't break down as often. Edgers hate it when stuff breaks down.

17. **They forgive quickly.** They don't hold a grudge and

would rather get on with the future rather than mulling over the past. Their ability to forgive quickly shouldn't be confused with them being naïve.

18. **They check in.** Not interfering, just making sure that things are as they should be. This habit comes more from wanting things to be right rather than from a fear that things are going wrong.

19. **They give a positive response.** This is one of the key habits of all people with the Edge. It starts with simple responses to questions like, 'How are you?' Those with the Edge are rarely 'not bad' or 'fine'. They're 'great', 'wonderful' or 'brilliant'. Even when a situation occurs where it would be very easy to be negative they find a way to communicate the same information in a more positive way. For example, where others might say, 'This is a nightmare,' they would say, 'This situation could be a lot better.'

20. **They read.** Edgers read something every day. Usually material that makes them better.

There are dozens of other habits that could have been listed. You may not agree with my entire list. I chose these habits because they keep coming up again and again. Have a quick review and see how many you have.

4

Values for Life

You may not agree with them but it's difficult not to respect a person who lives their life based on a set of core values. And, in the main, most Edgers do. What's interesting is that it's their ability to articulate those core values, make decisions using them and live by them that sets them apart.

Could you articulate your top ten values to me right now? And, if you could, how well are you doing living by them? As easy as it is to write them down, articulate them and even believe that you live your life by them, the truth is that most people experience a conflict of values on a daily basis. To find your Edge I really do believe you have to find, understand and live by your core values. Yet very few people actually take the time to understand what their values even are, never mind examine how they are driven by them, make decisions based on them and why they feel thoroughly miserable when they contradict.

Edge-It

To find your Edge you have to find, understand and live by your core values.

UNDERSTANDING YOUR CORE VALUES

Apologies if you are one of a very small group of people who have done this before, as I'm going to ask you to do it again. I'm sure you'd like to think one of your values is openness, so you'll be fine about me asking you to go through a whole values process a second time. If you've never done this before, you're in for a treat!

Before we get started I must credit my friend Tim Brownson for giving me so many ideas on how to share this process; he is quite the genius. To make this as easy as possible I'm going to break it down and fire in comments as we go. It will take you about ten minutes and you WILL need a pen and paper or a photographic memory.

Step One: Your Current Values

Take a moment to write down your current values. STOP. Before you do this, remember this is a list of your CURRENT values, not what you'd like your values to be. Here's what most people do, and as you're not most people I know you won't. Most people write down a list of the values they want or aspire to rather than taking a good honest look at themselves and writing down the values they actually have. Don't worry, we will get to the ones you want in a minute but, for now, write down your current values.

To help you consider what your current values might be I've created a hints list to help you. You may want to start with this list and just tick the ones that apply to who you are now.

Success	Authentic	Passion	Greed	Equality
Enthusiasm	Happiness	Humour	Significance	Trust
Power	Integrity	Recognition	Control	Blame
Honesty	Humility	Rejection	Excitement	Love
Security	Gratitude	Leadership	Persistence	Peace
Worry	Positivity	Kindness	Knowledge	Growth
Spirituality	Contribution	Health	Creativity	Fun
Fairness	Family	Commitment	Forgiveness	Freedom

You'll notice there are a few in there that might be considered undesirable, such as 'Greed'. The truth is we all have a few values of the sort that Tim Brownson brilliantly describes as Anti Values. Greed is a classic one. You don't think you have it but when the buffet's announced you're up there like a shot packing your plate in case they run out of sausage rolls and crinkly crisps. No one else is going to see your list, so be honest and have a go at writing down your top ten values now.

Edge-It

Most people write down a list of the values they want or aspire to rather than taking a good honest view of themselves and writing down, not the values they have, but those that will transform them.

Step Two: How Do They Help You Now?

Now that you've written your list (you have written your list?) ask yourself how easy it would be to live your life based on these values. Will they help you to find your Edge? Do they take you further from it or will they have no effect?

OK, that's the easy part – if you've done it. And you have done it, haven't you? I mean, I can't believe you would get to such an important part of this book and just keep on reading rather than doing the exercise. Oh, you'll do it later; fine. Add procrastination to your list!

Step Three: Creating a Hierarchy

Now you need to work out your hierarchy of current values. So take a couple of minutes to put them in order. I know they're all important, but have a go at numbering them from one to ten. If you're unsure how to do this with a list of ten, just compare two at a time and you'll eventually work it out. One more thing: values can be complex so don't start analysing at this stage, just get them written down.

Now stop for a moment and consider this. You have just joined a very small percentage of the population who have actually considered what their current values are, written them down and put them into a hierarchy of importance.

Step Four: Dealing with Internal Values Conflicts

I'm assuming you've got your list and put your values into some kind of order. Here's where they can become a little more complicated, especially when you end up with values conflicts.

Values conflicts occur when you have valid but potentially opposing values on your list. So, for instance, you have 'fun' and 'vibrant health' on your list. You go for a night out with friends and end up having four gin and tonics, a bottle of wine and a couple of bottles of beer, before finishing the night with a pizza. That was fun, so you can tick that box. Now how does that fit with your value of vibrant health? The next morning you wake up with a stonking headache, you step on the scales and immediately feel worse. You wish you hadn't gone so crazy last night. It wouldn't be so bad if it was a one-off but it's happening a couple of times a month now. You've had a values clash and that's why you're feeling like you've let yourself down.

Here's another classic: 'success' and 'family'. You know that having a happy family is a success, but you're not going to win *employee of the month* with that one. Now you're torn between doing what you need to do to get to the next level in your career and wanting to leave early on a Thursday to take your kids to drama class.

Values-driven Edgers know how to get the balance right. They've often consciously worked hard on their hierarchy of values and in the majority of cases they stick with it. They know that staying focused on living out their authentic values is what makes them truly happy.

Edge-It

Values-driven Edgers know how to get the balance right.

Step Five: Making Values-based Decisions

The next time you're faced with an internal values conflict ask yourself where in your hierarchy the values come, and make your decision based on which is the higher value. Making decisions – even the really tough ones – is much easier with a strong set of values.

When I was nine and my brother was ten we got a new headmaster at our junior school. One of his first decisions was to change the venue for the Christmas parties. In the past they had been held in the Methodist church hall, but the new headmaster decided that they should take place in the function room of the local Working Men's Club. Many of the parents didn't like the idea of this and several threatened to say so, but only one did anything about it. My Dad.

He called the new head, introduced himself, and asked if he

thought it was appropriate to have a party for seven to ten-year-olds in a room where the weekend before they would have hosted a blue comedian and lunchtime strippers. He went on to question the suitability of a venue that would stink of old smoke and have a bar. The new head laughed at my dad and said, 'Don't worry, they won't be serving drink.' There was no way he was going to change his mind, so my Dad wrote him a letter which simply said that my brother and I wouldn't be attending the Christmas party.

I remember the day of the party vividly. Kids came to school all dressed up and the talk (as it had been all week) was about the party. At lunchtime my Dad came to the gates of the school and when everyone else walked to the Victoria Social Club we walked home. I didn't understand; my eight-year-old brain just didn't get it. I tried my best to hold back the tears but I couldn't. I blubbed all the way home.

It was several years before I really understood what my Dad did that day, but once I had worked it out I couldn't have been prouder. My Dad stood up for what he believed in and made a tough choice based on values. Many years later I talked to my Dad about that decision and how hard it must have been. He told me that the decision had been easy; knowing what to say to his little boys was the hard part.

Edge-It

It's hard to make difficult values-based decisions. It can be even harder trying to explain them.

Step Six: Using and Abusing Values Filters

One of the challenges we all face is that we view the world, and other people's behaviours, through our own set of beliefs and values. Busy people can't believe that some folk can watch TV for six hours a day. Religious fanatics struggle to understand that there may be other beliefs and ways to worship other than theirs. Rather than altering your filter it's much easier just to assume that people with different values to your own are wrong, stupid or even evil. That's how wars start. We may think that wars happen because of other reasons but at the end of the day it's down to the values of one nation, group or person being opposed to another's.

Edgers with brilliant values know this so they take time to understand another person's values first. They rarely impose their values on others, preferring to live by their own and simply trusting that others may see them for who they really are. Of course, this is an attractive trait.

Edge-It
Edgers take time to understand another person's values first.

Step Seven: Projecting Values

No one likes having another person's values thrust upon them. If anything, it makes you more determined to hang on to your own values rather than being open to another's. The values don't have to be political, religious, corporate or anything serious; sometimes it's the little things. Have you ever met a smoker who's quit or a fat person who got thin? Suddenly, because their values have changed, they want to impose their values on others. And they're the good ones!

What about greedy people who feel that their behaviour will be more acceptable if they can get others involved?

I'm not suggesting you don't give your opinion: just keep in mind that your values may not be the same or exhibit the same hierarchy as those of the people around you.

Step Eight: Changing Your Values

Can you change your values? YES! Of course you can.

Take a moment to consider the person you ultimately want to become. With that description, identify the core values and the hierarchy of that person. Once you've done that, you can take a look at your current values and ask what needs to change.

I've carried out this exercise hundreds of times with coaching clients and in workshops. It really is one of those exercises that creates 'aha' moments for those who are prepared to participate in the process.

I like to challenge people during the process by pointing out potential conflicts between their vision of who they ultimately want to be and their values. These are a few of my favourites:

I want to live to be a hundred. Or I want to achieve all my goals.
Do you have 'Health' on there?

The Edge

I want to experience everything the world has to offer.
Might 'Adventure' be a value to have above yours of 'Security'?

And one of my favourites:

I'm known for my humility.
Do you think 'Success', 'Recognition' and 'Fearless' might need to come down your list just a little?

It's worth taking more than a fast five minutes to really get the best out of this exercise. Edgers spend hours consciously and subconsciously looking at their values and how they live their lives by them.

Edge-It

When you rewrite your values you rewrite your destiny.

5

Don't Curb Your Enthusiasm

There's only one thing worse than having no enthusiasm and that's having too much of it! People with Edge know where their enthusiasm meter (enthuseometer) turns red and have an uncanny ability to keep their enthusiasm high enough for people to feel it but low enough for it to stay just below the red line.

So what enthuses you? Genuinely enthusiastic people are a pleasure to be around. They can take the dullest subject and make it come to life. Teachers, scientists, even train spotters can take the boring and make it breathtaking. A recent example of this natural and controlled enthusiasm could be seen on British television when physicist Professor Brian Cox brought record ratings to the BBC with *Wonders of the Solar System* and *Wonders of the Universe*. Millions of people, including me, were glued to their TV sets as he made concepts such as the second law of thermodynamics come to life in a way that meant we didn't just get them, we were enthralled by them.

Yes, he's an expert and of course a general understanding of the second law of thermodynamics helps. But it's hard enough just trying to understand that stuff, never mind explaining it in a way that helps eight million viewers to get it. But what Professor Cox does brilliantly is to mix his expertise with his enthusiasm in a way that becomes totally engaging.

WHEN TOO MUCH IS TOO MUCH

I love the US TV show *Curb Your Enthusiasm*. In many ways the title is the antithesis of what the show's about. Larry David's character often shows loads of enthusiasm ... just for the wrong things. It's cringe-worthy and fantastic. When he was asked about the title of the show, Larry David explained that it reflects his perception that many people seem to live their lives projecting false enthusiasm, which he believes is used to imply that 'they are better than you'.

None of us would like to think that our being enthusiastic would cause others to think we're trying to be better than them, which is why we have an in-built enthuseometer.

USING YOUR ENTHUSEOMETER

It's built in, it's switched on, it's finely tuned and ready for action. We all have one, so why is it so many people don't listen to theirs? Let's give your enthuseometer setting a range of 0–100. Think about your average day and gauge where your enthuseometer will be reading.

Alarm clock goes off	1_____100
Getting ready for a new day	1_____100
Commute	1_____100
First task of the day	1_____100
Meeting	1_____100
Lunch	1_____100
Problem passed from your boss	1_____100
Presentation to a client	1_____100
Home time	1_____100
Workout at the gym	1_____100
Cooking a meal	1_____100
Eating the meal	1_____100
With a wee glass of something	1_____100
Watch the news	1_____100
Go to bed	1_____100

I'd be surprised if you gave all of those a high score. It would be totally unnatural (and a bit freaky) if you went through your life with your enthuseometer measuring 100 all of the time. What's most interesting for me is what the Edgers do. As much as they, too, have their ups and downs of enthusiasm, they do tend to start from a higher base line. Their questioning mind and internal dialogue is constantly judging their level of enthusiasm. They know that if they've dropped below an optimum point, the point where they are at their best, they need to adjust it.

Edge-It

Edgers, too, may have their ups and downs, but their enthusiasm tends to start from a higher base line.

Consider a time or event in your life when you have felt so enthusiastic you'd easily have scored high 90s on the enthuseometer for hours or days at a time.

The reason I asked you to recall or replay something you've felt genuinely enthusiastic about is that it's almost impossible to respond to the simple instruction, 'Be more enthusiastic.' We all know that, so why do so many people ask us to do it?

For some people being enthusiastic is associated with effort. The truth is that being enthusiastic alleviates effort. What state of mind would you rather be in to tackle a tough sixty-minute workout at the gym? Enthusiastic or lethargic? What's the best way to start a new project? Enthusiastic or indifferent? What type of leader would you rather be? Enthusiastic or apathetic?

HOW TO CREATE ENTHUSIASM

I was going to call this section *How to create enthusiasm when there's little to be enthusiastic about,* but searching for a situation where there's 'little to be enthusiastic about' is a challenge. Well it is for me. Maybe it's about mindset? Remember, you get what you focus on; if you choose to focus on not being enthusiastic you'll find little to be enthusiastic about. Which brings me nicely to the first step towards increasing your enthusiasm.

FIND SOMETHING TO BE ENTHUSIASTIC ABOUT

It really doesn't matter what, just find something. Even if you need to go into your past to remind yourself how it feels to be enthusiastic, you'll find something. I'm a naturally enthusiastic person about most things, but if you were to ask me to go back in time to a point when I was at my most naturally enthusiastic about anything, I know exactly where my mind would take me. To the summer of 1980, when I was thirteen. This was during the long hot school holidays (they were all long and hot back then) when most boys of my age were growing out of 'childish stuff' and when, with the help of my two best mates at the time, Stuart Cook and Robert Savage, I built a rope swing. I was so enthusiastic about that swing that it was all I could talk about. When I should have been sleeping in until lunchtime I was out of bed first thing, over the fields and down to the swing. I had the time of my life. I can still feel the energy, excitement and pure raw enthusiasm of that time in my life. For you it probably wasn't a rope swing; it may be the day you started a new job, met the love of your life or made a commitment to change something that you felt passionate about. Whatever it was (or still may be), see if you can remember that feeling now.

Edge-It

Maybe there is something you're incredibly enthusiastic about right now, or something you're enthusiastic about for your future. Do whatever it takes to get that wonderful feeling of enthusiasm into your body.

Even if your 'thing' or subject may seem boring to others it's worth considering how you can engage people in a way that they really get it. Take Economics. For most of my life I avoided Economics at all costs. If the subject came up in conversation I'd find myself looking for the nearest exit. How anyone could actually study it, make a career out of it or write about it beat me.

That was until I read *Freakanomics* by Steven Levitt and Stephen Dubner. Suddenly I was enthused by Economics because they enthusiastically shared why Economics affects everything.

Here's a question for you. How do you *do* enthusiasm?

What do you focus on? What are you aware of? What do you do with your body? Are there any key words that come to mind? Do you find it easier to be enthusiastic about something from the past, the present or the future? Take a few seconds to feel it. Your enthusiasm DNA is beginning to be unlocked and once you find your key to being enthusiastic it's much easier to be fired up about anything.

Edge-It
Enthusiasm is a virtuous virus; you can't spread it unless you've got it.

Edgers know how to be enthusiastic and they also know how to bring out the enthusiasm in others. Enthusiasm is a virtuous virus; you can't spread it unless you've got it. You can infect people with your enthusiasm; everybody, even if they've been vaccinated with the dreaded enthusiasm antidote: indifference. Do you know, I'd rather spend time with a really negative miserable pain in the backside than with someone who's indifferent. At least you know where you are with them.

Edge-It
The indifferent are cold, unmoved and dull. Never be indifferent.

Let's get back to the Edgers and what they do to be enthusiastic. I know it sounds like a personal development cliché but they look for the bits to be positive and enthusiastic about. By thin-slicing the bigger situation, then focusing on the bits about which they can be enthusiastic, they quickly find it easier to be enthusiastic about the whole event.

The Edge

I could be more enthusiastic about going shopping with my wife, so I thin-slice the whole experience and focus on the bits I can genuinely enthuse over. We'll probably have a nice lunch, she'll love it and I love to see her happy. I'll pop into the Apple store, etc. Quite quickly it's possible to be much more enthusiastic about any situation when you break it down and focus on the best bits.

It's simple but not easy. In fact it's much easier to thin-slice and focus on a negative. I once heard a person who had VIP concert tickets and back-stage passes for one of the hottest acts around complaining because it would be difficult to park and they might have to go to the multi-storey 500 metres away! Amazing. Alternatively I've heard someone being so enthusiastic about losing their job, choosing to see it as a positive, an opportunity to grow, that I employed them.

Young or old, male or female, whatever your race, colour, religion, size or shape, your enthusiasm will have a bigger impact on how others react to you than almost anything else. Getting the balance just right is the key. Too much and you're OTT, too little and your apathetic. Listen to your enthuseometer, focus on everything you have to be enthusiastic about, and spread the virus.

Edge-It

Your enthusiasm will have a bigger impact on how others react to you than almost anything else.

6

Edge
Etiquette

They could be considered arrogant but instead they're recognised as confident. They could be pushy but they choose to be polite. They could be loud but instead they listen. They could self-promote but instead they self-deprecate. Edgers know how to behave.

I don't want to name-drop (you'll see why later in this chapter) but to recount this story I'm going to have to, to set it up. One of our friends is the TV presenter Davina McCall. One February night we were having dinner with Davina and her husband Matthew in London. As we left the restaurant a young homeless guy came up to us and asked if we could please give him some money. Quick as a flash Davina pressed a note in his hand and asked him if he had somewhere to stay that night. Mid-sentence he recognised her: 'Hey, it's Davina isn't it? Can I have your autograph?' Amazingly, between the five of us we didn't have a pen or a piece of paper so Davina said, 'Sorry I can't give you an autograph, how about a hug instead?'

Then she hugged him for a good fifteen seconds. 'There, how's that?' she asked.

'Better than an autograph,' he said.

I've seen Davina do that kind of thing on many occasions. No fuss, no cameras, no discussion afterwards, just doing the right thing.

I'll not waste time with stories of what I've seen other less-well-known 'celebrities' do or not do. Is it about confidence? How you were brought up? Core values? Probably a combination of them all with a big chunk of self-awareness thrown in.

Edge-It

While interviewing Edgers for this book, there wasn't a single person who didn't have impeccable manners.

I read an article some years ago based on research around what made people referable. It was one of those commonsense pieces backed up by a survey of a few thousand people. The basic question they were answering was: why would you recommend of refer someone? The article then went on to identify the top three habits of those who are most easily referred. One and two weren't earth shattering: 'Do what you say you are going to do' and 'Do things on time'. It was number three that stood out. The most common habit of people who were regarded as highly referable was that they always said 'please' and 'thank you'. It wasn't as general as 'they were polite'; it was very specific. They always say 'please' and 'thank you'.

Edge-It

Top Three Referability Habits:
Do what you say you are going to do.
Do things on time.
Always say please and thank you.

When I read this research I was thrilled. I do what I say I'm going to do, I do things on time and I was sure I always said 'please' and 'thank you'. It turned out that I could have been a lot better at saying 'please' and 'thank you'. I knew I was better than most but I wasn't brilliant at it. I could make up loads of excuses but the truth was I often missed my 'please' and, worse still, my 'thank you's' (as a close friend pointed out).

This is where you need a coach, an honest Joe who'll point out when you've missed a 'please' or forgotten a 'thank you'. And who better to do that for you than your husband or wife.

The Edge

Well, anyone really! I asked my wife to point out every time I forgot to say 'please' or 'thank you'. The rules of this challenge were simple. In private she would point out there and then if I missed one. This would be for every interaction, from making a cup of tea to being told the road was clear at a junction. In public she would either give me the 'look' (I think all men know what that entails) or she would point out the omission to me afterwards. And I wasn't allowed to say, 'I was just about to . . .' or claim that I had said 'please' or 'thank you' but she hadn't heard me.

The first few days were the most challenging; as with going to the gym, the first few times are the toughest. Again like going to the gym, you can quickly begin to resent your trainer when you think you're doing your best but they want more from you! After a couple of weeks, though, I really thought I was making progress. It was time for a review (I was actually hoping it was time to stop). Coach Christine did a classic praise sandwich. 'Yes, you're much better. You say "please" and "thank you" a whole lot more than usual.' Then the meaty bit: 'However . . .' – don't you just hate the however – '. . . there's one area where you still need a lot of work.'

'Tell me,' I demanded. I wanted three out of three referability habits and if I was close I wanted to know. Damn it, I needed to know.

'Well, there are three people who you still have a long way to go with. Me and the kids.'

Ouch, that's not what you want to hear. The people who are your nearest and dearest, who should get the very best of you, get a second- or third-rate you instead.

A couple of the Edgers we interviewed invited us into their

homes. It was interesting to see the way they interacted with their partners. Being grateful, kind and generally pleasant was a habit, not a chore.

Edgers may not know the impact they have on others, but they do know that every interaction creates an emotional correlation between them and the person they are interacting with.

At a conference a couple of years ago I was asked to be a part of a panel discussion. Audience members would fire questions and two or three members of the panel would give their responses. One of the panel members was a particularly fierce woman. I'm not sure why but she seemed to be angry about everything. One of the questions was around advice for saving time. I have a real interest in this subject so I was interested to hear what the other panel members would say, especially the fierce lady. The panel gave the usual mix of doing the important stuff first, having a clear plan and knowing how to delegate; then it was the turn of the angry lady. 'I cut out all the fluff. If it's unnecessary I don't say it or do it.' The chair of the panel asked her for an example, and her reply offered a brilliant example of what not to do.

'If I receive an email I read it on my Blackberry. And if I need it printed I forward it to my PA with the word "Print". I don't have time for anything else. She knows what I mean and when I get back to the office it's on my desk.'

I wasn't sure if I was the only one who found this response interesting, so after the discussion I asked a couple of fellow panel members if they would ever send a one-word email like that. All said the same. They wouldn't. One added, 'I write an email in the same way I talk to someone face to face.' Could you say the same? Please, take a look at the last ten emails you sent to people in your team. Would you speak with them face to face in the same way?

Edge-It

Write emails the same way as you talk to someone face to face.

The behaviour of the Edger is, as you would expect, exemplary. But this model behaviour doesn't come without a cost. Because Edgers are expected to behave in a certain way, the second their guard drops and their standards slip it sticks out like a sore thumb. I have to admit that I enjoy a glass of wine at an event, but the more I've studied Edgers the more I've considered how I behave in public. Many Edgers don't drink in public at all because they know that after a couple of drinks things change. And if you're wondering what that looks like, cast your mind back to that evening when you were invited out for dinner and you were the only one driving, not drinking. The champagne and wine begins to flow. Everyone else starts to relax, lighten up and eventually slur their speech. In their minds they are exactly the same person who sat down three hours ago. You, on the other hand, feel like a genius, listening to their rapidly deteriorating conversation.

The humility of those with the Edge is one of their most redeeming features. They're not shy, meek or lacking in confidence but they are humble and modest. Subtle differences. Humility is such an attractive trait, so why don't more people practise it? It's probably down to a combination of lack of confidence and pride.

Edge-It

Humility is such an attractive trait, so why don't more people practise it?

Here's where my whole Edge theory could potentially go belly up. What about Lord Sugar; he's not always polite. And Piers Morgan: I doubt you'd describe him as being humble. I can only answer by going back to the point I made at the start of this book. It's about finding your Edge. If you think it's OK to belittle people and bulldoze your way to the top regardless of the wake you leave behind then that's your choice. You won't be on my Christmas card list but I guess I wasn't on yours. And that's the point. You'll attract more of what you are. So if you decide that you want to be arrogant, or greedy or rude, expect to find a lot of people like that in your life. If you'd like to be surrounded by people with humility then read on.

Below are some of the characteristics that make the humility of Edgers so special.

CREDIT OTHERS

Edgers go beyond the simple credit where credit is due. They actively give others recognition for the contribution they make to their personal success – and they don't wait until Oscar night (or an equivalent award ceremony) to do it. It's regular and direct.

AVOID FALSE MODESTY

Some people confuse humility with false modesty. I know someone who will cook all day, prepare the most amazing meal for others and then, when you compliment them, they say, 'Oh, it's just something I rustled up.' Do that at work and you'll have your boss thinking, 'Hmm, what could they achieve if they put some effort in?'

PUT IT ALL DOWN TO LUCK

Edgers will often comment on how lucky they feel to be in the position they are in and enjoying their success. They'll say it's down to many factors, the work they put in being at the bottom of the list. We've all heard the famous quote by Gary Player, 'The more I practise, the luckier I get.' His way of saying, if you work as hard as me, focus on your game as much as I do and have the same steely determination that I have, then you might, just might, be as good as me.

In a nutshell it's not how lucky you are, it's what you do with your luck that makes the difference.

DO WHAT'S EXPECTED

And don't make a big deal out of it. Peter Beardsley is my favourite-ever footballer. He played for Newcastle over three hundred times and scored more than a hundred goals. He won the hearts and respect of everyone in football. Not because he was a flashy player but because of his incredible work ethic. He would often cover 25 per cent more distance in a game than any player in a similar position. He played with style and was always graceful in defeat. When he was asked about his incredible work rate he would simply say, 'I'm just doin' me job.' Compare that with current players earning £200,000 a week who spit the dummy out and refuse to play because of a childish disagreement with their manager.

AVOID ONE-UPMANSHIP

My dad's bigger than your dad should have been left in the playground years ago, but was it? The fact is that most people courting one-upmanship aren't even aware they're in the game, and that is the danger. Could your enthusiasm be mistaken for a bit of bragging?

It starts with little things: a sarcastic comment or a foolish comparison and, before you know it, it's game on. Maybe a, 'Oh you're going there for your holidays. That sounds nice, but if you go away again I'll tell you where you should go . . .'

PARK THE PRIDE

Pride gets in the way of humility. By holding on to pride you invariably end up telling people what it is you're proud of. Get two people in a room who are caught up in personal pride and the focus will quickly turn from being proud to how to outdo each other.

LET PEOPLE HAVE THEIR MOMENT

Everyone likes to have a moment of glory, so allow people to have it. Even if you do know a funnier ending to the story or know for a fact that they've got the details muddled up, don't dive in.

ADMIT WHEN YOU'RE WRONG AND TAKE IT ON THE CHIN

There will be plenty of times when you're wrong. And there will be times when people just can't wait to point it out. Take it on the chin, gracefully, thank people for their feedback and, if need be, apologise. This is a hard one, especially when criticism may be given in the wrong way or with the wrong intent. The humble will reflect, the arrogant will defend.

BE INTERESTED (RATHER THAN INTERESTING)

Get out your old Dale Carnegie books and brush up on this one. Mr Carnegie, and a thousand others (including me), have written about it, research has proven it and you have experienced it: you'd rather spend time with people who are interested (in you) than people who believe they are interesting (probably to themselves).

Edgers tend to perform these soft skills effortlessly; they are very much part of their DNA. The good news for the rest of us is that we can brush up on or learn these habits and behaviours through a bit of openness, an honest Joe and the desire to be just that little bit better.

7

Deal or No Deal

My wife and I had a meeting with a financial advisor – and yes, it was as grim as it sounds. However, an interesting part was when he asked us how averse to risk we were. I said I was quite open to risk and Christine said she didn't consider herself a risk-taker; she's generally more

cautious than I am. 'Then let's see!' the FA announced. He took great delight in explaining that his company had spent a huge amount of money and thousands of hours developing a questionnaire that would identify how risk averse we really were.

So we set to work scribbling and scoring ourselves against various scenarios and situations. We measured our beliefs, fear of loss, age, income, current levels of saving and a dozen other factors before handing in our work. A few moments later the FA was ready with our results. I'll not reveal the exact outcomes for fear I'll be deluged by financial advisors from across the country who'll no doubt have the perfect portfolio ready for us, but I will tell you the one thing that really shocked me. When it comes to money, I'm significantly more risk averse than my wife. The main reason I was taken aback is that many years ago we agreed that she would look after all of our finances . . .

Edgers approach risk in a slightly different way than most people. Yes, as you would expect they are more open to taking risks; no surprise there. What fascinates me is why?

Edge-It

The Edger's attitude to risk is unlike most people's.

Here's a question for you. If you take more risks will you be more successful? Just for a moment, imagine you have your entire life savings in a box. You can double everything in that box and all you have to do is correctly predict the outcome of the flick of a coin. There's a 50/50 chance. Would you go for it? My guess would be no. So let's change the parameters. Same box, same life savings, but this time you have a dice. If you throw the dice and get any side other than a six you will double your money. If you land on a six you lose the lot. So the chance of you losing your hard-earned cash is one in six (about 17 per cent) and the chances of you doubling your life savings is now five in six (about 83 per cent). Now what would you do?

Now I'll add the dimension you've been waiting for. You can bet a percentage of your life savings; you don't have to go 'all in', but you can only make this bet once.

We all do a slightly different calculation at this point, which depends on one thing: the size of your comfort zone. The size of your comfort zone has a huge impact on your level of risk. And comfort zones can grow or shrink based on multiple factors.

Edge-It

The size of your comfort zone has a huge impact on your level of risk.

EXPERIENCE

The more experience you have the bigger your comfort zone? Perhaps, but is that the case for an author? In fact, the more experience you have the more readers expect, the more readers expect the greater the pressure, the greater the pressure the bigger the risk, the bigger the risk the greater the fear. This is my sixth book by the way.

On the flipside, experience helps with risk taking. The more experience you have the better you become, the better you become the more confident you feel, the more confident you feel the happier you are to take a risk and step outside of your comfort zone.

The number one factor that stops people from stepping out of their comfort zones is fear. Fear of failure. Fear of what people might say and think. Even fear of getting it right and having to do what you've done again. Edgers are brilliant at dealing with fear. It's not that they don't have fear; they do. It's how they deal with it.

Edgers know that not all the fears associated with risk are real. They're able to filter them and rapidly assess what's real and what's imagined. Most people exaggerate what's imagined and then search for the proof that backs up why they shouldn't take the risk. Eighty per cent of new businesses fail! Now there's a heartening statistic for the self-employed. An Edger reading that statistic doesn't just think, 'Excellent, that means 20 per cent will succeed and I'll make sure I'm in that 20 per cent.' They analyse what the 20 per cent are doing, apply that acumen to their business and massively reduce their risk of failing.

Edge-It

Eighty per cent of new businesses fail! An Edger reading that statistic thinks, 'That means 20 per cent will succeed.' They analyse what the 20 per cent are doing, apply that acumen to their business and massively increase their opportunity for success.

Returning to our meeting with the financial advisor. After we'd completed our detailed and quite boring risk assessments I suggested his organisation could have saved a fortune in design costs and done something which was much more enjoyable: we could have taken part in *Deal or No Deal*. You'll probably be aware of the premise of the programme so I'll skip the bit about explaining rules and get straight to it. How can people make such foolish decisions?

Did you know that you are 20 per cent more likely to think your horse will win a race if you have a bet on it? That's because you're in the game. You have an emotional attachment to the outcome so you believe you're going to be luckier. It's the same with *Deal or No Deal*. 'The banker would like to offer you £31,000 for your box, Sandra; deal or no deal?'

'Well Noel, the quarter of a million is still out there, so it's no deal.'

The crowd go nuts. Brave Sandra chooses three more boxes.

First box. It's blue, £100, and Sandra, the crowd and her fellow participants go crazy.

'That was a good choice,' counsels Noel.

The next box ... it's the £250,000. A massive groan from around the studio followed by polite applause and a faint shout of 'Go on Sandy' from Sandra's husband Jim, who's just seen his trip to Barbados and Porsche Boxster fly out of the window.

Sandra leaves with £250, consoling herself that she came with nothing, had a great time and met some really lovely people who she'll definitely keep in touch with.

Edgers wouldn't get on *Deal or No Deal*. The producers would weed them out in the interview process. Edgers know £31,000 is a lot of money. They know how hard you have to work to net £31k after tax and they know that even though they came with nothing they sure as hell aren't going home with nothing.

Edge-It

When Edgers do take a risk they know three things: exactly what they are risking; what the chances are of a favourable return; and, most importantly, how they will handle the situation if it should all go wrong. And it's their ability to handle the consequences that really sets them apart.

Last year we went to Las Vegas. It was our first visit so we asked friends who'd been for some advice. Most friends suggested we set aside an amount of money each day for gaming and work on the basis that if you lose it it's gone and you won't worry about it. We naïvely thought $100 a night would be enough. Precisely eight minutes after I sat down at a Black Jack table I'd lost all of my money (and remember, I'm the risk-averse one!). For some folk that could be seen as a bad start. I was tempted to dip into the next days' $100 to 'get back in the game' but I didn't. Instead I just people-watched for a couple of hours. I think you can learn more about a person's attitude towards risk and money during two hours in a Vegas casino than you can filling in endless risk assessments. Most people pop into a casino for a bit of fun but others are unbelievable. I watched one guy playing roulette who repeatedly put $250 on a single number. That's a 37/1 chance with a payout of 35/1. Each time he didn't win he was devastated. On the same table were a young couple who would bet $10 on black or red each spin, and they were having a great time.

Let me be clear: I'm not saying the guy at the table was right or wrong. It would be amiss of me to suggest that he's repeatedly failing, the same as it would be wrong for any of us to suggest that taking any risk is a failure if it goes wrong. The part that fascinated me was his reaction to the consequences and then his choosing to repeat his actions, time after time.

So what happens when something that involves risk confronts us? We didn't expect to find ourselves in a certain situation, but once we're in it, then what? We can still choose how we feel about it.

And this is the biggest differentiator between those who

have the Edge and those who don't. Edgers spend little time considering how they got into an unexpectedly risky situation and a lot more time working on how they are going to deal with it.

Edge-It

Edgers spend less time considering how they got into the crocodile's mouth and more time working on how they are going to get out of it.

A couple of years ago while we were on holiday I met a fascinating chap who claimed to be an expert on how to survive a plane crash (Christine thinks I attract them!). I thought this guy was intriguing and worth having a beer with, particularly when he offered to share some of the traits plane-crash survivors have in common.

First of all, most believed they would live. Now I appreciate it's difficult to know what the mindset was of those who didn't make it. Maybe they thought they were going to live too. However, the chap I was talking to argued it was much more than that. Survivors would describe some people being frozen to the spot, in shock and not knowing what to do, whereas the survivors made decisions, took action and wasted no time.

They also kept uncannily calm; almost to the point of seeming robotic. No screaming, hysterics or panic, just a meticulous, conscious action towards safety.

Edge-It

Survivors remain uncannily calm with no screaming, hysterics or panic. They make decisions, take action and waste no time.

Afterwards, they would recount how they almost felt in a state of 'flow': being able to focus on exactly what they needed to do, backed up by their ability to do it.

Knowing how to turn inaction into anticipation or fear into fascination is what will give you the Edge in any situation. And I can guarantee you that the more you find your Edge the more likely it is that occasions will arise where risk will be thrust upon you. Your ability to make a decision and act on it will be vital. And don't worry, you're unlikely to be in a plane crash; you'd stand a far greater chance of winning £250,000 in *Deal or No Deal*.

8

Asking Great Questions

Edgers are in a constant dialogue with a very important person. This person gives excellent advice and also advises them when they should ask others questions. That person is themselves. Not really surprising, as most people talk to themselves most of the time. Don't you? What's different for the Edger is the quality of the

dialogue they are having. In order to get the very best answers, they ask themselves better questions.

Edge-It
Edgers are in a constant dialogue with a very important person – themselves.

Sometimes the questions are asked at a conscious level, even written down and considered. Other times the questions are merged into a conscious and subconscious internal dialogue. This throws out answers that other people might consider to be random thoughts and ideas but Edgers know to be part of their thinking process.

Think about the questions you ask yourself most often. You may want to write them down, as they'll reveal a lot about you. Then consider the list below. How do these questions compare to the ones you ask of yourself?

Thirty questions Edgers ask themselves:

1. **What will make this better?**
   This is one of the most common questions. The quest for continuous improvement prevails.

2. **How can I change this?**
   Sometimes things need to change. Where most people think 'I wish this were different' the Edger asks how can they change it.

3. **Where now?**
   Whether it's expanding their business or planning a trip, the question evokes action and demands an active response.

4. **If there was a way, what would it be?**
   The question after the question. This often comes to mind when other avenues appear to have been exhausted. It promotes creativity and encourages the thinker to move out of their box.

5. **Why hasn't anyone done this?**
   Sometimes this is asked through frustration when an Edger wonders why people they know, employ, live with, etc., haven't done something that they see as common sense. Also asked when they spot an opportunity.

6. **How can I communicate this?**
   There arc many ways to communicate a message. This simple question gives the possibility to consider alternatives and find the best way.

7. **Who do I know who . . . ?**
   This question is a great way to tap into the mental 'little black book'. And it's not just about immediate contacts; it's easily expanded to 'Who do I know who knows someone who . . . ?'

8. **What's the worst that could happen?**
   Richard Branson's famous 'Screw it, let's do it' saying is often followed by this question.

9. **What if it works?**
   A great flip on the naysayers who love to think about what could go wrong.

10. **Where would I find . . . ?**
   In an age where knowledge is king this question takes you beyond a Google search and makes you look further.

11. **Can I/we do this faster?**
   Everyone wants stuff faster these days. By asking this question you can become aware of ways to shave seconds, minutes, hours and days off a timescale.

12. **How do I feel?**
   An opportunity to check in and see how the most important person in the world is doing.

13. **How does this make others feel?**
   This is a great question to help with self-awareness and the impact your actions may have on others. Listen carefully after you've asked this one.

14. **When will I exercise today?**
   It's not surprising that Edgers ask this question a lot. It's easy when you're busy not to look after yourself. By asking this question you begin to mentally schedule time to work-out.

15. **How can we reduce the cost?**
   More than ever, people are focused on costs. By shaving time and money off your outgoings you can have a tidy impact on the incomings.

16. How can we increase the profit?

Turnover for vanity; profit for sanity. The bottom line is what counts, so after you've answered question 15 this feels naturally like the next place to go.

17. Is there a better way?

This is a question that constantly runs through the mind of the Edger. Even if it's got nothing to do with them, they still question the status quo and ask themselves if they can think of a better way.

18. Has this been done before and, if so, by whom?

Success leaves tracks. The chances are that someone somewhere has information that can help you.

19. What do I need to prepare?

Edgers love to be prepared. They ask themselves this question a lot. Even if they don't need all the information, the feeling of going into a situation fully prepared fills them with confidence.

20. Is this sustainable?

While others are getting excited about a break-through, the Edger is already two steps ahead. Amongst many other things they want to know if this is a flash in the pan or something sustainable.

21. Who can help me?

There are millions of people who are just waiting to help out and millions more who need some help. Edgers ask themselves when faced with a problem:

who will be best to help them? Invariably, the right person comes to mind.

22. What would [INSERT HERO OF YOUR CHOICE] do?

A simple way to consider other angles, make decisions based on values and generally give your thinking a whack. Although I say 'insert hero', that's just to get you started. Edgers will consider their competitors, parents, dictators; in fact anyone who will help them with their decision-making process.

23. Is that true? Do I really believe in this?

When something seems too good to be true it's usually because it is. Edgers question facts, the media, others' opinions and even their own beliefs.

24. Does this fit with who I really am?

A values-based question that can save a lot of time and heartache later. Listen to your intuition after you ask this one.

25. Is this enough?

It could be you ask this because you need more or it could be because you've had enough. This is an anti-greed question that can make you a happier and healthier person.

26. Can this be scaled?

Scalability is in the forefront of the minds of the investors on *Dragon's Den*. You may think you're thinking big, but they're thinking bigger!

27. How long will this take?

Because Edgers value every minute of their precious time they're not frightened to ask how long something may take. The difference between folk with the Edge and others is that Edgers pose the question whereas the others just keep checking their watch, hoping for something to end.

28. Who could do this for me?

A key question when it comes to delegation. Edgers are constantly thinking of who could take on a responsibility or task to allow them to go on to the next thing.

29. Is this transferable?

Taking one idea and moving it to another discipline, country, culture, etc. is the goal of many entrepreneurial Edgers. They also think about what skills they have that can be transferred to others and what skills they would like to have transferred to them. What do you want to transfer or have transferred to you?

30. What's the message?

Being able to simplify a message is an art. Edgers ask this question because they never rely on others knowing and understanding the message. Think like a PR and marketing guru and ask yourself what you're really trying to say.

Now you've been through the list, are there some questions that jump out at you because you already ask them of yourself? Are there some that you've thought about but don't ask nearly as often as you could? Are there a few that you've never considered before, but that you can add to your questioning arsenal?

Asking questions is easy. It's the quality of your questions that is most important. Did you notice 'What's for tea?' and 'What's on TV?' didn't make it? For some people asking powerful questions is easy, it's a natural skill. For others it's more of a challenge. However, it's a skill that is simple to learn with a bit of brain training.

Edge-It

Asking questions is easy. It's the quality of your questions that is most important.

You can print this list out from 'The Edge' pages on my website, www.michaelheppell.com, and use it as a simple resource. When you have a few minutes, just run through the list and use your live issues as the context.

Are you going to do the exercise? What will make you do it? When will you do it? How will you know it's working? What will you add to the list? I know you'll find it useful to do this. Do you?

9

Dealing with Setbacks

I remember watching the repeated attempts by Richard Branson to circumnavigate the world in a hot air balloon.

I think he had four attempts in all, which either had to be abandoned or, in one case, didn't even get off the ground. I think you'd have to agree that Richard Branson is one of the more famous

Edgers; he's renowned for daring acts and taking risks.

The thing that always fascinates me about Sir Richard is the way he deals with setbacks. He never looks angry, often refers back to them with a kind of affection and clearly has no regrets. Now, the cynics would say that it's easy for Richard Branson to act like that because he's so successful. Actually I think he's so successful **because** he acts like that.

Richard Branson is no stranger to setbacks in business and in his personal life. There's no need to feel sorry for him and he wouldn't want us to, but we can learn from how he brilliantly deals with setbacks.

WHEN BRANSON BITES BACK

1. He never goes down without a fight. He'll try anything to cling on, tackling governments, other companies and the system to get what he's after.
2. When it's time to quit he gets out. Even though he could afford to, he doesn't fall in love with ideas that mean he throws good money after bad.
3. He looks at every failure as a brilliant learning opportunity. Read his autobiography and you'll see.

Even when his home on Necker Island was destroyed by fire, his attitude was quite remarkable. Yes, he's probably well insured and can have an even better house built to replace it. But he lost his notebooks – irreplaceable. He lost thousands of photographs – irreplaceable. I mentioned this at a corporate event recently and a cynic remarked that he didn't care if Richard Branson lost his photographs or notebooks. 'Hasn't he got enough already?' Fair enough, that's his belief.

Sometimes the world has a strange way of making a point. At lunchtime I watched this same guy run back into the seminar room and start to rummage through his bag. He looked flustered and harassed. I asked him if he was all right. 'Not really,' he snapped, 'I've lost my f***ing phone.'

The old Michael Heppell would have had a field day with that one; however, I'm a little older and a lot wiser, so I just smiled. Wouldn't it make a great story if he had looked back at me, had a moment of clarity and said, 'Ohhh, yes Michael, I get it,' but he didn't. He continued frantically tearing through his bag before accusing the hotel of nicking his mobile. Of course he found his phone; his friend picked it up because he was worried his pal would lose it.

Edge-It

Edgers have hundreds of setbacks. Yes, they feel them. Yes, they hurt. But they learn from them and quickly move on.

The Edge

There are hundreds of examples of successful people who have failed repeatedly on their journey to success. These are a few of my favourites.

Henry Ford – After two failures, The Ford Motor Co. was his third business.

Steve Jobs – Kicked out of Apple.

J.K. Rowling – Harry Potter was rejected by twelve publishers.

Walt Disney – Fired by a newspaper editor for lacking ideas.

Soichiro Honda – Turned down for an engineering job by Toyota.

Thomas Edison – Told by his teacher that he was 'too stupid to learn anything'.

Michael Jordan – Dropped from his high school basketball team because of his 'lack of skill'.

Simon Cowell – Goes bust, moves back in with his parents and is told he can't be successful in the music business.

John Grisham – Rejected by sixteen agents and twelve publishing houses.

Stephen Hawking – Developed motor neurone disease while studying at Cambridge. Some suggested he would be unable to complete his degree.

Oprah Winfrey – Fired from her job as a television reporter because she was 'unfit for TV'.

Fred Astaire – Received a memo from the testing director of MGM saying 'Can't act. Slightly bald. Can dance a little.'

Alex Hayley – His novel Roots received 208 rejection letters.

And one for luck:

Michael Heppell – Told by his English teacher, 'Michael is a waste of time. He will never do anything with the English language.' Perhaps she was right?

I asked dozens of Edgers the exact question, 'How do you deal with setbacks?' What follows is a summary of their typical responses.

SHORT TERM

It Still Hurts – Just for a Shorter Period of Time

Of course Edgers feel the pain of an idea going belly up or of an outright rejection. A famous actress shared with me that she feels sick when she doesn't get a part. But the day she doesn't feel anything will be the day she quits acting because the flipside is the thrill when she does get a role. The difference, she told me, is that 'I don't sit and dwell on it for weeks; I'm over it in about a day now.'

I Don't Take It Personally

That's a tough one. Because it *is* personal. Edgers just know how to compartmentalise their feelings a little better. Many use self-talk to do this.

Edge-It

Edgers know how to compartmentalise their feelings.

I Ask, What Have I Learned?

OK, so I didn't get the job/the project failed/it's the end of the relationship, etc. What have I learned? Great Edgers don't just reflect after a knock: they write it down and actively learn from setbacks.

I Change the Time Frame

'How will I feel about this one week, one month or one year from now?' That's a common way Edgers think about setbacks.

I Stay Positive

Easier said than done? Well, not if you've practised being positive. If your natural state is a positive disposition then it's much easier to get back to that state when you hit a challenge. The advice is simple: practise being positive when you don't need to be, so that you'll remember how to do be positive when you do.

Edge-It

Practise being positive when you don't need to be, so that you'll remember how to be positive when you do.

I Take Action

Next! By focusing your attention on what's next and taking action towards it you feel better about the setback. From simply picking up the phone, to moving your body, having a conversation or reading something inspiring, you'll move the emphasis away from the challenge.

LONGER TERM

I Ask Myself What I Can Do with What's Left

By being resourceful, Edgers know that they can often turn the remnants of a problem into something positive. Examples range from Edison's famous discovery of five thousand ways not to make a light bulb to Piers Morgan being sacked from his job as editor of the *Daily Mirror* and going on to host his own show on CNN.

Edge-It

Edgers have an uncanny ability to turn what's left into a valuable asset.

I Stay Vital

After a big knock it's easy to stop looking after yourself. You'll have another drink because you deserve it. After all, you've had a hell of a day. Sod the gym – I'm having a pizza! Edgers tend to turn that on its head. They flip the disappointment into motivation and focus on feeling great in themselves. I know one Edger who, after losing his business, went on a retreat, learned how to meditate, became a vegan and lost 40 lb. When he came back to Britain and started his next venture (which was a great success) he commented that the reason his first business failed was that he had been tired, stressed and bloated.

I Surround Myself with the Right People

Having the right people around you is essential. The 'I told you so' bunch are far too clever to say those exact words, so they disguise their glee at your failure with knowing looks and innuendo. But you still feel it. Spend time with people who want to see you do well and will be happy to see you back at the top.

Being hit with setbacks, experiencing failure, feeling that everything is going wrong and it's the end of the world, are emotions felt by everyone with the Edge. So if you've had those experiences and feelings, congratulations, you're in fine company.

Here's to failure!

10

Keep Calm and Carry On

You'll get what you think about. And an Edger's focus is laser sharp.

Isn't it fascinating when you meet a real pessimist? I'm talking about a hard-core doomster whose entire focus is on what's wrong, what could go wrong and what's already gone wrong. You've got to admire someone who can carry that amount of negativity and still exist. Although they would probably say they're going to die soon anyway.

Please don't think I'm about to say you should be an eternal optimist. There are times when a little bit of pessimism may just save your life, your business, your relationship or your job. It's all about the balance. I carried out a bit of scientific research (i.e. posted on Facebook and Twitter) to find out what people thought the optimism to pessimism ratio should be for success.

The results were an overwhelming 4:1. Surprise surprise: the 80/20 rule; Pareto would be proud.

What do you think?

What do you think the Edgers believe?

This is a big 'it depends' question. And it differs depending on your type of 'Edge' and what you need it for. If you're in the military, a pinch of pessimism will encourage you to plan a better strategy, but if you're focused and fighting for your life, then park your pessimism.

If you're in sales there are very few occasions when the pessimistic mind works best. If you're involved with risk assessment and scenarios for disaster then go for it and be as pessimistic as you like – just don't tell me about your worst-case scenarios: I'd rather not know.

What I did find was that those with the Edge never go below a ratio of 2:1 optimism to pessimism and mostly operate at around 4:1 or even higher. That's 4-plus optimistic thoughts or actions for every pessimistic one. With that type of focus you'd have to create an optimistic view of the world.

Edge-It

Edgers have more than four optimistic thoughts or actions for every pessimistic one.

Another question for you. Where do Edgers put most of their focus: the past, present or future?

Edgers have the ability to focus on two places at once: the present and the future. They spend little time focusing on the past. The past is mainly useful to reference relevant experiences and gather data. Pessimists dwell on the past, reference it and quite often try to live in it.

The ability to live in the now but visualise and decipher the future enables Edgers to take the correct action. Edgers focus on very specific points in the future; they don't try to predict what will happen in ten or twenty years but instead their focus is on creating their future in six to twelve months. Compare this with how the majority of people think. Their view of the future has been heavily influenced by sci-fi (no, we won't be walking round in silver suits and eating a neutro-tablet for lunch) and their 'now' is punctuated with a desire to move things back to how they were. This pessimistic view stagnates people very quickly.

Edge-It

A pessimistic view stagnates people very quickly.

Edgers focus on what's right, especially with people. It's an optimistic trait that can land them in trouble, but they would rather start a relationship with a new friend, colleague, member of staff, etc. with a focus on what's right rather than on what's wrong. It's easy to focus on what's wrong with someone; they're human so there will be lots of evidence. It's much more difficult to focus on what's right.

Did you, like me, read *The One Minute Manager* by Ken Blanchard, and, if so, were you completely taken by Ken's concept of 'Catch people doing something right'? It's a brilliant concept that encourages people to focus on getting the best out of their team. Remember, Edgers look for the best in people.

Some years ago I worked with a division of HSBC Bank which had a brilliant leader called Irene Dorner. Irene is one of the greatest Edgers I've ever met. She went on to run many other divisions and territories of the Bank. While working to take the North of England, Scotland and Northern Ireland Division to number one in the UK performance ratings, Irene recognised that she needed to find a vehicle to show all 4,500 of her staff that they were doing something right. The idea we devised together was simple but brilliant. Irene bought 4,500 thank-you cards and announced (very publicly) that every member of staff would receive a card at some point over the next ninety days specifically referencing the great work they had done.

She then sold 4,485 of the cards to her direct reports and area managers. The fifteen she retained would be sent to the same managers over the following ninety days. The area managers followed the model and the cards cascaded to team-leader level. Each time the cards were sold the money raised was given to charity.

Over the next ninety days several interesting things happened. First, the people who had been doing a brilliant job received their cards quickly. It wasn't difficult for the managers to catch them doing something right, write their card referencing this, then hand it over.

Then the ones who had been doing a good job (not brilliant) started to raise their game and hint heavily to their bosses that they were working very hard. Some were a little more subtle than 'Hey look at me – when do I get my card?' but others were very direct. This all worked well because some colleagues who had previously 'played small' were now feeling much more confident about celebrating their success.

The really interesting shift occurred with the final group. Not only did they start to wonder when they were going to get their cards but the focus of their managers changed towards them. Rather than seeing them in a negative light the managers had to refocus and find something positive these people had done so that they could be given their card. This meant more coaching, feedback and skills training to help them step up. The pressure was on and the ninety days were ticking by. No one wanted to give or receive a card after the campaign had ended.

The cards were an outstanding success. Managers built bridges with troublesome team members, employees felt recognised for the work they were doing, plus several thousand pounds was raised and given to local charities.

Edge-It
Catch people doing something right and thank them.

When stuff goes wrong, those with the Edge turn their focus to fixing. This instinct prevails in sports stars and business leaders, but it's particularly prevalent in the military. Military

Edgers have an amazing ability to think clearly in situations where others would be frozen in a blind panic.

I went paintball shooting once and within ten minutes of going 'live' became a blithering wreck who didn't know his left from his right and his up from his down. I was relieved to be out of the game fairly quickly and retired with a nice cup of tea. Great military minds are trained to carry out tasks under stressful conditions so that when the training is over they can rely on reacting with the correct stimulus response. The challenge for most of us is that we're not trained to react properly to cancelled planes, losing important information, or unruly kids. Our reptilian brain kicks in and that's when fretting replaces fixing.

But there are three things we can all do to be a little more prepared for our moments of panic.

PRACTISE MEDITATION

Now I don't want to go all new age on you here, but if you've ever studied anything about meditation then you'll know that the benefits are amazing. Its results are long lasting too and not just limited to the time it takes to practise the techniques. So take a deep breath and relax . . .

RUN SOME SCENARIOS

Do you check where the fire escapes are and make sure you know the layout of a hotel when you check in? I'm not talking Jack Bauer schematics, just a general idea of where everything is so that it's relatively familiar to you should you need to get out quickly. Do you have an action plan to put into play should you lose your best client? Do you have an idea of how you would manage if your two best members of staff left? Do you have a Plan B should legislation change and adversely affect your sector?

BREATHE

Have you noticed how you breathe when you're in a panic compared to how you breathe when you're calm? Don't allow a situation to dictate your breathing; change your breathing and you'll instantly feel different about the situation.

Edge-It

Remember the Edger's secret; you get whatever you focus on:

Focus on being happy and you're more likely to feel happy.
Focus on being sad and you're guaranteed to achieve sadness.
Focus on what you want and you're more likely to get it.
Focus on what you don't want and you may get that too.

An Edger knows that laser focus consumes energy. Focusing on the wrong thing takes just as much time and energy as focusing on what's right. It's all about your choice.

11

Health on the Edge

How are you feeling? No, really, how are you feeling? Take a moment to scan your body from the top of your head to the tips of your toes. As you become aware of your body and how you feel, you also become aware of how you would like to feel.

I'm typing this page after six hours of writing. I've just taken a minute to scan my body and, guess what, it told me something. It was a simple message but nevertheless a clear one: 'Adjust your seat and get a cushion.'

Edge-It

Your body knows what it wants and, if you ask it, it will tell you.

Your body is brilliant. Just think of the abuse you give it and still it keeps you moving, allows you to experience the wonders of the world and has very simple needs (especially compared to your emotions or behaviours). My friend Dr Fiona Ellis taught me a very simple way to think about your health: eat well, think well and move well. She believes (and I agree) that everything comes down to those three areas of focus.

Let's take a look at them:

- Eat well. I'm sure you know all about this one, but do you? Really? It's more than having your five a day and counting calories. When it comes to having the Edge with health it's worth seriously considering what you put into your body. Read the labels, find out what they mean and be aware of what you eat. See Chapter 12, 'The Mental Edge', for more on this.
- Think well covers mental health, attitude, beliefs and mindfulness. Again, see Chapter 12 for more ideas.
- Move well is about keeping your body in a peak

physical condition. Yes that means exercise, and yes that means building your strength, but it also means stretching, having a massage, seeing an osteopath or chiropractor and a host of other move-well activities outside of hammering the gym.

When it comes to priorities, those with the Edge always prioritise health. It's crazy not to. I'm busy so I'll eat crap. I've got a lot on so I won't relax. I'd miss my favourite TV show so I won't exercise. It looks so stupid written down, but that is how so many people lead their lives. It's simply an excuse not to do the right thing.

Everyone knows prevention is better than cure yet still the temptation is to put off the most important area of work: working on your own health. I could rant for pages on this but instead I'll share seven of the keys I discovered from the Edgers who really care about their health.

1. Ultra hydrate. But don't drink all the time. Basically this means drinking lots of pure fresh water but giving your body a break – a couple of times a day – from processing liquid. I used to believe that you should sip water all day until the brilliant Derek Talbot asked me why. 'Because that's what you should do?' I suggested. Derek calmly pointed out that your kidneys might need a little rest every now and again. Simple thinking wins again.
2. Prioritise sleep. It's an absolute nonsense to think you can have the Edge without enough sleep.

There may be the odd exception where an Edger only needs four hours a night but the reason you hear about that is because it is an exception. Most people need more. You'll know the right amount for you. So programme it and do it.

Edge-It

Most people are sleep-starved and find themselves feeling tired at some point every day. Don't be most people.

And getting to bed earlier is the best way to do it. No TV, no stimulants (coffee/tea/Coca-Cola etc.) and no drama. Just slow down, read a book (this one) and drift off into a deep relaxing sleep.

If you find it difficult to sleep, read the section on Mental Architecture in Chapter 12. You can also download relaxation music and guided visualisations that will help you to nod off and have a better-quality sleep. Go to my website www.michaelheppell.com for some suggestions.

3. Allow recovery time. And by recovery time I'm not talking about the time when you are asleep. This is about giving yourself great breaks, a chance to unwind, an opportunity to focus on a pleasurable activity and time to recharge.

This time gives you the energy to do everything else you want to do. I suggest you treat these days like you would any other important day in your life and schedule them.

4. Listen to your body. Your body is giving you information constantly on what's needed. Just as a great mechanic can listen to an engine and know what's needed, you should be able to do the same with your body. When you get a hunch about something, ask your body what it needs. It could be dehydrated or lacking minerals or vitamins. It could be stressed or exhausted. Ask, listen and act.

5. Be open to opinion but trust yourself. For every one opinion on your health there are a dozen others to conflict, complicate and contradict. Those with the Edge will always listen to opinions but ultimately they trust themselves.

6. Prevention is best. I know I mentioned this earlier but you and I both know this is the truth. What's thirty minutes of exercise four of five times a week compared to a major illness? How does saying 'no' to an extra portion compare to feeling fat and exhausted? If you don't want to take preventative measures for your own sake then do it for your family, friends and those who care about you.

7. It's constant and never ending. How many times have you heard people say, 'Are you on a health kick?' This, by implication, means you'll do something for a while, then go back to your old ways.

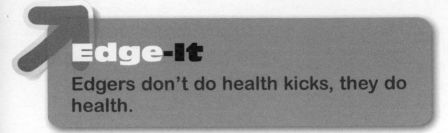

Edge-It

Edgers don't do health kicks, they do health.

12

The
Mental
Edge

You could argue that having the Edge is all about the mental process. Everything starts with a thought. However, there are some things that Edgers do that allow them to access more of their brain, enable them to think in different and more creative ways, and keep them sharp.

If I were to list all of the ways Edgers use mental techniques you would either be bored by their similarity or intrigued by the impact of the slightest nuance. I'd hate to risk boring you, so here's the key that, when applied, will give you a mental edge.

THE ABILITY TO HAVE A CLEAR MIND

Flippin' heck, that's a tough one to start with. A clear mind! What are the chances? Well, I know the answer to that. Having a totally clear mind with no distraction is impossible. Even the great masters of meditation will tell you that it is impossible to clear your mind completely. However, it is possible to have a spring clean.

The secret is not to try to clear your mind. As soon as you become aware of the fact that you are trying to clear it, your mind becomes focused on that task and subsequently you move further away from having a clear mind. Now that's a challenging one to get your head around!

The secret to having a clear mind is brilliantly explained by Andy Puddicombe in his book *Get Some Headspace*. He suggests you imagine yourself sitting at the side of a road with a blindfold on. You're aware of all the traffic passing, the noise and the stress, but you can't see what's causing it. When you start to meditate it's like taking the blindfold off your mind. You become more aware of the traffic; in other words, of your specific thoughts – positive, negative, helpful and stressful.

As soon as you start to go for that meditative state it's like trying to run into the middle of the road and control the traffic. Instead of helping us to relax, the meditation can actually cause stress. Andy suggests that you hold your seat on the side of the road and just get used to the flow of traffic, simply allowing your thoughts to come and go. As you do this the amount of traffic (thoughts) on the road starts to decrease and the space between the cars begins to increase.

When I was doing my research for this book I found that most Edgers know how to quieten their minds but not many are really sure how they do it. That's what I like about Andy's work: it's a 'how to' approach that anyone can use.

Edge-It
Allowing your brain to think less often helps you to experience more.

Another way that Edgers use their brains better is in the way they observe the world. Where others just plough on, Edgers are different. They see what others don't, hear what others can't and feel their environment in a special way. This applies particularly to the small things.

The next time you are taking a walk in the country with a friend or family member stop them and ask, 'What do you notice?' They'll probably say something like, 'The path' or 'The trees'. 'It's autumn which looks nice.' Ask someone with the Edge and they'll answer along the lines of, 'The air, it's so clean. The trees are beautiful; multiple shades of orange, yellow and brown. The birds are singing – at least three species, maybe four. The temperature is cooling by a degree or so since the clocks went back. We've been walking for just over an hour now. I can smell the remnants of fire from the gardens over there mixed with the moss from the woods.'

Edge-It

They see what others don't see, hear what others don't hear and perceive their environment in a different way. Edgers notice everything.

Here are four challenges for you:

- As soon as you have read this paragraph put down the book and notice your environment. Study what's around you. Allow your brain to fixate on items that bring back memories. Look up. What do you see? What can you hear? Which sounds evoke feelings and why? What's in the air? Close your eyes and really feel your surroundings. Who's near you? What relationship do you have with these people? What are they doing today? Are you hot, cold, just right? Take a few minutes to take in your environment. Do it now.

- As soon as you can, go for a walk and really notice what's around you. Use all your senses. Look up, down and all around. Slow down and listen. Identify the smells and tastes in the air and feel the surroundings.

- Listen to a piece of music and identify the

instruments. Focus on the lyrics of a song and what they may mean. Focus on the inflection of the vocalist and imagine the emotions they want to convey with their song.

- Really taste food. Start with how it looks. Take a moment to see what's on your plate: the colour, texture, shapes and sizes. Then smell it. Do this slowly. When you take a mouthful, really taste the food. Use every part of your mouth. As you chew, think about the flavours, textures and sensations. What do you like best? Why?

Edge-It

The more you exercise your brain the more aware it becomes. It's like going to the gym. The first few times it can be challenging but after a short while it becomes a habit – a good habit.

Edgers also know what to do with the negative emotions that others often hold on to. The ability to park destructive emotions is very powerful and plays a huge part in mental and physical health.

Only one person I interviewed was able to express exactly how she parked negative emotions, and her technique was fascinating. Whenever she was faced with a challenging or destructive thought she began by thanking her mind for giving it to her. Already she's ahead of the game. When did you last acknowledge and thank your mind for a negative thought? We normally try to suppress such thoughts and by doing so give them a new power. Next, she would take a moment to consider the thought and what it meant. If she was able to do something about it she would mentally file it in her 'To Do' box. I asked if this was visualised as a real box? With a surprised look she said, 'Of course; why wouldn't it be?'

If the thought concerned something outside of her control she would visualise it turning into a bird and flying off into the distance. Of course the thought wasn't totally gone but the impact of it was significantly reduced. More importantly, if it came back she would just repeat the process, and each time it would become easier.

Compare this with how most people dwell on negative and destructive thoughts, allowing them to take over.

Edge-It

The more relaxed and clear your mind is, the better it operates. Your quality of sleep improves; your ability to make decisions and your level of well-being also significantly improve. It's a virtuous circle.

MENTAL ARCHITECTURE

Edgers also do one more thing that enables them to access parts of their minds that lie dormant in others. They use their mind to create mental architecture.

This idea was first explained to me when I attended a course run by Jack Black (the Scottish motivational speaker, not the American actor), in which he shared the concept of taking your mind to a deeply relaxed state and mentally building a house on the bank of a river. The house would have rooms that could be used to do different types of 'mental programming'. I found the idea fascinating and studied others who used similar techniques, including a walk along a path, a trip into space(!) and revisiting your childhood. I developed my own model called White Island, which involved creating a beautiful island with features such as a spa, meeting area and bedroom.

All of these ideas use the same common theme, which is to quieten your mind, usually to a low Alpha state (very relaxed). Once relaxed you create the equivalent of a physical environment in your mind. The benefit of this is that it allows your mind to focus and create mental hooks on which you can attach your own thinking.

For example, if you have difficulty sleeping you would use your mental architecture to create a comfortable bed. While in your relaxed state you would see (and feel) yourself climbing into the bed and falling into a deep and peaceful sleep.

Athletes use a similar method to create their own running tracks, courts and arenas where they can mentally practise and prepare before a race, game or match. Tiger Woods became the master of this on the golf course. Some people claim to be able to treat their illness or even the illness of others using this method.

What will you create using mental architecture? A place to work, to be creative and make decisions? How about somewhere to refresh your physical body? Do you want to improve your golf? Then maybe a place to practise your swing or your putting would be of use. How about a planning studio where you can see your ideas and test new concepts?

The only limit is your own imagination.

13

Edgeucation

Education doesn't give someone the Edge but it can certainly enhance it. The challenge is: what type of education?

Any caring parent will tell you that they fretted over which school to send their children to. Some work on the fact that if you pay more you will get more, others move miles rather than risk a postcode lottery.

When it all works out, parents pat each other on the back, congratulating themselves on their wise choices. When it doesn't, it's the school's fault.

It is interesting how schools do the same. When

The Edge

a child is troublesome teachers can't wait to get them through (or out of) their school as quickly as possible. If a child is successful they are held up as a glowing product of their establishment.

A couple of years ago I was asked to be guest of honour at my old school's prize giving. Looking for inspiration I pulled out my final school report and quickly realised that my former English teacher had given me all the material I needed.

In preparation for the evening event I collected copies of my five best-selling books (including a No. 1 bestseller) published in twenty-two different languages. After I was introduced I walked onto the stage and produced my final school report. This was the report I was supposed to hand to potential employers, and as a sixteen-year-old I'd believed it to be a very important document. I turned to the comment written by my former English teacher – mentioned in Chapter 9 (page 109) – and read out her words: 'Michael is a waste of time. He will never do anything with the English language.'

I then commented, 'It's funny, isn't it, how a teacher can claim to know what the future holds for a sixteen-year-old by spending just two hours a week with them. Now, I know your teachers wouldn't do that. I'm sure they are incredibly supportive, but back then that's what my teacher said about me. And do you know what? I almost listened to her. She was very old then; her name is Miss L*******n. I bet she retired years ago.'

A hall-full of teenagers started shouting. 'She's still here! She's still teaching.'

Of course, I knew she was, and perhaps it was a little childish of me to set it up like that, but after twenty-six years I still couldn't help myself from wanting to get one over on a teacher.

Almost everyone I've met who has the Edge has a story of

144

how they challenged education. No matter how good their school was or how brilliant were their teachers, they all pushed the boundaries. It wasn't because they didn't want to learn; it was usually because they weren't fully engaged.

> **Edge-It**
>
> When Edgers challenge education it's almost certainly because their mind is being under-utilised.

Those with the Edge have a thirst for knowledge that takes them far beyond what conventional education offers. And It doesn't end after they finish their formal education; they just keep on learning.

> **Edge-It**
>
> Your brain needs to be nurtured and exercised just like your body. The difference with your brain is that the more information it consumes, the fitter it gets, whereas your body . . .

I believe that our education system could be much more effective at teaching young people how to learn. We under-use technology, thinking techniques, and multiple intelligence models. When the average eighteen-year-old's education is complete they rarely leave school with a thirst for more knowledge. They're mostly thinking, 'That's it, I'm done. Now it's uni, a job, or if I can blag the money from the parents I'll have a gap year.'

Meanwhile parents are thinking, 'That's it, they're done. Now get off to uni or get a job but don't expect me to pay for a gap year!'

Even university, which should be an amazing journey of discovery and learning, has become more about the money than the excitement of more education.

Edgers think differently. While it is true that most of the people I interviewed for this book do have a university education, it's also true that the vast majority believe their thirst for knowledge has become stronger over time.

Two notable examples of people who dropped out of college but never stopped learning were a couple of geeks named Bill Gates and Steve Jobs.

Bill Gates dropped out of Harvard after two years. Thirty years later he was given his (honorary) degree. During his acceptance speech he said, 'I'm a bad influence. That's why I was invited to speak at your graduation. If I had spoken at your orientation, fewer of you might be here today.'

Steve Jobs dropped out of Reed College after just six months. He found the structure difficult and his parents found the fees hard. He did, however, take a calligraphy class that nurtured his love of fonts. This knowledge became the basis for the amazing Apple fonts that were originally used on the Macintosh.

So can you learn how to learn? Can you acquire the knowledge of how to acquire the knowledge? I think so.

Here are the key habits that all lifelong learners have in abundance.

1. Always read. Most of the Edgers I interviewed were reading a minimum of two books at any one time. All had a library with a large stock of books and they all subscribed to and read industry-specific publications.
2. Look outside your sector. This is a must. Who else is doing what, why are they doing what they're doing and what does it mean?
3. Use multiple forms of education: reading, online, TV, events, courses, audio learning and, most importantly, conversations.
4. Ask better questions. One of the Edgers I interviewed, Jack Krellé, asks brilliant questions. By doing this he challenges his brain to see situations from multiple angles. His views are fluid; his opinions are constantly forming and reforming as he gathers more information. It also makes him a fascinating person to spend time with.
5. Reflection. My father used to say to me, 'Now son, what have you learned?' It's a great question. Many people keep a journal, which is an excellent way to help one reflect. The best journal insights can come from answering that simple question: what have I learned today?
6. Openness to ideas and willingness to change. Who says that what you believe to be correct is correct? Shouldn't you be open to having your ideas challenged? A practice that is much easier to say than do. Who really wants to have their opinions challenged and their beliefs questioned?

7. Surround yourself with learners. If it's true (and I believe it is) that you become like the people who you spend most of your time with, then take a good hard look at the people with whom you hang out now. Do they have a thirst for knowledge or a thirst for the pub?
8. Prioritise learning. If it's important, schedule it. Some of the busiest people I know find the time to learn more because they schedule it. Create a learn file and fill it with knowledge you need to digest. Carry it everywhere.

Before you read any further, take a moment to consider these questions:

- What have I learned today?
- What will I learn next?
- How will I use what I'm learning?

Edge-It

Edgers never stop learning, and not just in a passive sense; they frequently go out of their way to learn something that's outside of their normal sphere of life.

14

Getting the Best Out of Your Advisors

Without exception, everyone we interviewed for this book commented on the importance of surrounding themselves with exceptional people. Whether this was as part of their paid team, paid advisors or well-meaning friends, they valued the input of others,

listened to their advice but always made their own final decisions.

What's most interesting is that they've always done this. Even before they were recognised as having achieved a level of success, they would still find a way to meet the best people to ask for advice.

When Napoleon Hill wrote the classic, *Think and Grow Rich*, he coined the phrase 'Mastermind Group'. By this he meant a special group of advisors brought together to work on a specific project. Their pooled intellect creates a focus and energy that combines to produce a far greater power than could be achieved by brilliant but separate minds. Of the millions of people who have read *Think and Grow Rich* I wonder how many have successfully created and used a Mastermind Group? It's far more realistic to create mastermind alliances with small groups of individuals who have a desire to help.

Edgers are masters at setting up these relationships and it starts with a trait they use constantly: the humility to ask. It's almost irrelevant whether the person whom they ask for help says yes or no. If it's a no, they'll quickly ask someone else. And because Edgers tend to have a wide circle of contacts, they have plenty of people to ask.

Edge-It

Edgers are masters at setting up Mastermind Groups. It starts with a trait they constantly use: the humility to ask.

There's a part of your conscience that is pre-programmed to help others. When someone asks you for help you're most likely to ask yourself, 'What can I do?', rather than shut down the conversation and say no. Edgers know this and, as well as knowing how to ask, they know what to do to keep you onside and helping.

Many years ago I worked as the director of a community foundation, a charity established to help people support their local community. One day my office received a call from Sir Tom Cowie OBE. Sir Tom lived just up the road and was well known for building highly successful businesses, one of which is now known as 'Arriva'. Arriva currently employs almost fifty thousand people and operates in twelve countries. Not bad for a bloke from the north-east of England who started with a motorcycle shop. My PA buzzed through with an excited tone, 'I have *the* Sir Tom Cowie on the phone for you Michael.' I'd probably met Sir Tom only twice before, so I was more than slightly surprised that he'd called me. I put on my best director's voice and took the call.

'Hello Michael, it's Tom Cowie here. I was just wondering if you could give me a lift to Newcastle?'

I'll just set the scene: here I am with a pile of work, in an office forty minutes from Newcastle, being asked by an incredibly wealthy businessman (who I know employs a chauffeur) for a lift to Newcastle. What would you say? And that's what I said too. An opportunity to spend some time with Sir Tom Cowie was too good to miss; everything else could wait.

Ten minutes later I was pulling onto his drive having changed shirts, buffed shoes, checked breath and carried out the fastest mini-car-valet in history. A couple of minutes into the journey I asked him why he'd called me, and he said, 'Because I needed a lift.' Brilliant! When Sir Tom needed something, he'd ask. We didn't get into why he wasn't using his chauffeur but we did talk about the importance of asking people when you needed something. As I was running a charity at that time, I needed donations. There was never going to be a better time, so, seizing the opportunity, I asked him to help the County Durham Foundation. He said, 'Yes.'

Super-successful Edgers do this all the time. They'll pick up the phone to anyone and build relationships with everyone. It's not about building a list of contacts, anyone can do that. Choose carefully which networking events you attend and avoid those where you're sure to leave with a bunch of business cards from people you'll never see or hear from again. It's about using the contacts you've made and being available to them in return.

Edge-It

Super-successful Edgers do this all the time. They'll pick up the phone to anyone and build relationships with everyone.

Building a list of professional advisors works in the same way; it's just that most times you'll need to pay for them.

MAKING SURE YOU GET BEST VALUE FROM ADVISORS

The more successful you become, the more people will offer you advice on how to achieve even greater success. Often this advice will be good. Sometimes it will be brilliant. And on occasions it will be dreadful. Edgers quickly separate the wheat from the chaff.

Here are a few things to consider when using advisors.

Take References

Of course they'll say they are good. Of course they'll show you brilliant testimonials (who wouldn't?) but if you really want to find out how good someone is, ask them for the names and numbers of three people who they have recently worked with. If they won't share this with you and instead start banging on about client confidentiality, maybe they've just talked themselves out of the job.

Get a Quote

Even if it's a 'guesstimate' you must get something in writing. More relationships with advisors are ruined because there's a lack of transparency over fees than for any other reason.

Ask for a Guarantee

This really sorts out the pro's from the 'having a go's'. Great paid advisors will be happy to guarantee their work. And their guarantee will be simple and stacked in favour of the purchaser. My guarantee is simple: 'If you're not 100 per cent

155

happy with the work we do we'll refund you 100 per cent of any fees paid.' This guarantee does two things:

1. It gives my prospective client confidence. One of the main objections to using a high-fee advisor is price. With a guarantee such as mine, there is no financial downside.
2. It keeps me sharp. I don't want to give my fees back so it ensures that my team and I are constantly working towards making any experience of working with us brilliant.

You may not garner a guarantee as generous as mine but you should be able to get something if your advisor really believes in their ability to deliver.

Edge-It

A guarantee needs to be simple and honest. And if someone takes you up on your guarantee, honour it swiftly with no fuss.

Use per Project

Sorry to all the consultants reading this who love the idea of a retainer, but Edgers rarely pay for professional advice that way. They know that consultants get lazy when they're on a retainer. When an Edger pays, they pay for the best.

Ask the Stupid Question

That's why you're paying them. Never be too embarrassed to ask anything. I once saw the chairman of a company ask a specialist consultant why she was working on a particular problem. 'Because you asked me to when we met last week,' she replied.

'Did I? Good. Well I'm pleased you remembered!'

Should They Become Arrogant, Fire Them

Yes, you want to be challenged, yes, you want them to do the stuff that you can't, but if they become arrogant get rid of them. We recently witnessed a company that had contracted a consultant on an eighteen-month retainer. His position was secure and he swanned around the organisation as if it were his own. The respect wasn't there, the consultant didn't fully buy into the vision, but the company felt there was little they could do about it. Painful.

Remember, They're Your Advisors

At the end of the day, they are advisors. They don't always know what's best and if they're good they'll welcome your feedback if you don't think they've got it right. Only people with a stake in the final outcome should make the final decisions. The next time a financial advisor suggests you buy a product, ask them first if they've invested in it.

Be Prepared to End the Relationship

Again, sorry to the consultancies whose primary purpose seems to be to get a foot in the door and then, once they are in and comfortable, keep on selling time, solutions, services or whatever.

The Edge

A brilliant consultant will do what I do (sorry to sound big-headed but read on). Whenever we enter into a project with an organisation we tell them at the outset that one of our goals will be to put ourselves out of a job. And we mean it. If we do our job well enough you shouldn't need us to keep coming back. We should have empowered your staff and given them enough tools, techniques and self-belief to do the job without us.

I met someone recently who told me they've worked with the same coach for the last eight years. When I questioned why he'd stuck with a coach for so long he explained that they had done such a great job in the first year and changed so much for him that he didn't feel like he could end the relationship!

One of my wonderful (former) coaches, Peter Field, said to me at our first meeting, 'Your two hardest decisions will be making the decision to start working with me and then making the decision to stop. If you can't make the second one, I'll do it for you.'

Share with Them

When you do find great paid advisors, look after them. Give them all the information they need to make the best decisions. Edgers know the importance of sharing knowledge to get the best results. First, ask your advisors to sign an airtight non-disclosure agreement, then share.

Be Clear

Be abundantly clear on the scope of the project and the results you are looking for. Let the advisor know how you will measure their success. I'm still gob-smacked when paid advisors think they've done a great job only to find they've been working on the wrong problem.

Working with paid advisors is great if you can afford to. And if I was pitching for your business I'd probably say that you can't afford not to. But the reality is, if you can find great advisors who are prepared to help you for free then why not?

I've written before about the four magic words to use when you want someone to help you. They're so simple but they are brilliant when used in the right way. They are, 'I need your help.' There's something about those words when they are said (not emailed or texted) in that exact order that makes people want to help you. I've tested out other combinations of words that mean the same thing, but nothing works as well as 'I need your help.'

Edge-It

The four magic words. **I need your help**.

So, imagine you need some help, you've found the person who can help you and you've engineered a situation where you are able to ask them. If you already have the Edge then securing a 'yes' without anyone needing much more information is the norm. If not, what's the first question anyone is likely to ask? 'What do you need?' or 'What do you want?' And this is where you had better know your stuff. The last thing you need at this point is any hesitation or lack of clarity. That will almost guarantee a 'Can I think about it?' or 'Can you put that in writing?' Which basically translates as, 'No, I don't want to help you – you confuse me. But I can't say no, so I'll just see if I can slow you down a bit.'

Asking for help in a clear and succinct way isn't always as easy as you think. When I started to write this book I really messed up when asking a couple of people for help by trying to explain too much in my initial request. 'I'm writing a book about how highly successful people continue to raise their game. My plan is to distil the information into a book that inspires others to find their own Edge. Oh, by the way, it's going to be called *The Edge* . . .' By that time, their eyes had started to glaze over. So I changed it. After 'I need your help' and their initial positive response I simply said, 'I'd like to interview you for my next book.' Some said yes straight-away, others asked questions, none said no.

Surrounding yourself with too many advisors can be as detrimental as having none at all. Once you have someone on board from whom you have asked for advice they will give it and keep on giving it until you ask them to stop. Multiply this by three, four or more and suddenly your life is more about deciphering your advisors' information and less about moving forward.

Edge-It

Two great advisors who know what you require, how long you require them for, why they were asked, and that you'll keep your side of the bargain, is all you'll need.

Finally, be prepared for payback. Be upfront with this and offer your help straightaway. And if your advisor should ask you for something, be prepared to go the extra mile and do whatever it takes to be brilliant for them.

15

Moving On, Moving Up

Do you remember the moment when you realised that you might actually be brighter than your teachers? Whether it was a parent, school-teacher, lecturer or boss, there's often that moment when you think, 'Hold on, I know more about this than you do.' I can vividly recall three moments.

163

The Edge

The first was when I was around eleven years old (1978) and a massive Electric Light Orchestra fan. I remember telling my dad that their concert featured all kinds of special effects, including lasers.

'They won't be using lasers, son,' he said, smiling.

'Yes they are. I've seen it on the telly,' I insisted.

'No, son. They may have looked like lasers but they won't have been lasers. Lasers can kill people so you wouldn't be allowed to use them at a pop concert.'

And that was the moment I realised that I knew more about lasers than my dad did. No big deal, but it made me question what else he 'knew for certain'.

The second big moment came when I was fourteen and 'studying' (being the loosest of terms) at Blackfyne Comprehensive School in a town called Consett, County Durham. In those days the boys did metalwork while the girls did needlework (sounds medieval, doesn't it?). Anyway, one day in the metalwork class one of the boys was using the oxy-acetylene welding equipment. He was so busy concentrating on the piece that he was welding that he didn't realise he had actually burned through the tubing carrying the acetylene. A huge yellow flame shot into the air. As one, the whole class looked first at the flame, then at our teacher. What happened next will stay with me until my dying day.

Our teacher started to run towards an open window, shouting at the top of his voice, 'FIVE SECONDS!' Next, he leapt through the window, did a barrel roll in the teachers' car park and crouched behind a parked car. Meanwhile, a classmate who was standing next to the welding bench simply walked up to the acetylene tank and turned it off.

The flame went out almost instantly and all eyes turned to the car park where our now-quivering teacher was bracing himself for the impending explosion. I cannot think of a time when I've laughed as hard and for as long. It was brilliant. And that's when I realised that at least one of my teachers wasn't that bright after all. I didn't even consider the fact that he looked after himself before his pupils.

Christine, my wife and business partner, remembers vividly the moment she realised she'd outgrown her boss. It was during a meeting with a very demanding client. They were working their way through a proposal when the client turned to Christine's boss and said, 'I have to say, this is the most comprehensive and well-presented brief I've ever seen.' And with Christine sat right next to him, he took all the credit for her work and said, 'Thank you.' Then, back at the office after the meeting, he told her that the follow-up materials had better be of the same standard as that's what the client expected from him. She knew more than him; he knew it but couldn't admit it.

Edge-It

It's easy to resign when you discover what your boss is really like.

Edgers frequently outgrow their teachers and also their friends and colleagues and siblings and neighbours and just about anyone else they have a relationship with. By their very nature, their desire to become better means that unless they have other people around them who either (a) want to do the same or (b) understand their desire and adapt, they will outgrow them.

However, what the Edgers do brilliantly is to ensure that if a relationship becomes too distant they don't fall out over it. They remember and respect what the relationship has given them in the past, and are able to remain positive and focus on that.

JOSE AND BOBBY

Did you know that José Mourinho started his career as a translator for Sir Bobby Robson? He first worked for Sir Bobby as his interpreter at the Portuguese football club Sporting Lisbon, but when Sir Bobby recognised his talent he promoted him into more senior roles. Mourinho followed Robson from Sporting Lisbon to Porto, and then on to Barcelona.

However, when Robson offered him an assistant coaching position at Newcastle United, he refused and took up a head coach role at Benfica instead. He'd outgrown his teacher. And, much as I loved Sir Bobby, you can't argue with the amazing success of Mourinho. He's won the league title in four different countries, won the Champions League twice and is generally regarded as one of the best managers of recent times.

He learned from Robson, absorbed knowledge and then, when he felt confident in his own abilities, moved on despite there being a much easier option available. Mourinho always respected and admired Bobby Robson and demonstrated this by donating his FIFA Ballon D'Or World Coach of the Year Award 2010 (the year he won the Champions League with Inter Milan) to the Bobby Robson Foundation, where it was auctioned for £26,000.

I wonder, if Mourinho had gone to Newcastle as an assistant would he still be known as 'The Special One' and would he have gone on to win that award?

LEAVING THE HIT FACTORY

Kylie Minogue released multiple singles with Stock, Aitken and Waterman (SAW). They were known as The Hit Factory for good reason: her first thirteen singles with them all went into the UK top ten. But when Kylie decided to leave SAW in 1992 the press, 'music experts' and even fans anticipated it might be the end of her singing career. And for the first couple of years it looked as though they might have been right. Her first album after SAW did all right, but nothing compared to the blockbuster sales she'd enjoyed earlier. Of course Kylie was exploring new ideas and collaborating with a range of different artists and producers. In 2000 she released the single 'Spinning Around', which hit the No. 1 spot in forty countries.

I recently spoke to Pete Waterman at Kylie's Anti Tour concert. He said, 'I was writing songs for Kylie before half of this audience were born. Boy, she's done well.'

Edgers know that they're likely to outgrow their teachers at some point, but they never write them off. Edgers know that great teachers will always be great teachers because they make them think. Occasionally you'll find a situation when a symbiotic relationship occurs: a teacher becomes an associate and you can teach them as much as they can teach you.

Edge-It

Edgers know that they're likely to outgrow their teachers at some point, but they never write them off.

Associations between a teacher and former pupil aren't made because the two think the same, nor because they are poles apart. They are made because their way of thinking complements the other's. When you find someone with whom you have this special bond you'll never outgrow them – they're one in a million. So if you've discovered such a person (or when you do), hang on to that relationship.

If you have outgrown a teacher and it's time to move on, you'll know. You'll have an overwhelming urge to find new knowledge, inspiration and experience. It's hard, especially if you respect and care for the teacher you're leaving, but you'll know when it's time and, in their heart, they will too.

16

The
Talent
Engine

Finding, nur-turing and developing talent is a high priority for anyone with the Edge. It's a myth that you can 'just buy talent'. First of all, there isn't enough out there and, second, to quote the MD of Red Carnation Hotels, Jonathan Raggett, 'Talent goes where talent wants.'

Edge-It

Organisations need talented people more than talented people need organisations.

Jonathan Raggett is an Edger with a passion for nurturing the best talent and, wherever possible, he wants to do it from within. Visit the concierge desk at The Chesterfield Hotel in Mayfair and you'll meet Chris. He has a cut-glass British accent, an encyclopaedic knowledge for what's happening in London and a charm that could entice the birds from the trees. Jonathan found Chris working in the hotel laundry. 'Within thirty seconds of meeting Chris I knew he had something special,' he told me. 'I'm constantly looking for talent and who knows where you'll find it?'

Like many Edgers, Jonathan Raggett is constantly seeking the best and it doesn't matter if the talent doesn't work for the Edger – talent likes to see talent grow.

Everyone knows that succession planning is important, but organisations rarely do enough about it. Everyone knows that if you don't develop talent you will lose it. The talent will leave you. Those with the Edge know this and spend extra time focusing on talented people.

This, of course, is in sharp contrast to those who feel threatened by talent. Rather than develop it they'll make sure the talent is firmly put in its place and kept a rung or two down the ladder.

A few years ago I was a director of a company that organ-ised leadership programmes. Most of these were good but there was one programme that shone brighter than any others. We called it the Talent Engine.

The concept was simple. Find talented people, bring them together and immerse them in a stimulating programme using the best trainers, coaches and presenters we could find.

A typical programme would look like this:

FIND THE TALENT

They could come from anywhere in the organisation, but mostly we found that organisations were nominating their bright middle managers.

INTROSPECTION

The next stage was to find out where they were in their lives and work, and to explore what type of person they were. We used a series of diagnostic tools (some better than others) to do this. What was most interesting was how engrossed the partici-pants were in their own results.

HOW TO BE BRILLIANT

Next, participants joined me for two days on a 'How to Be Brilliant' residential programme. We worked hard, running the first day from 9.00 a.m. until midnight and the second from 9.00 a.m. till 6.00 p.m. The idea behind two days of intensive learning was to make the participants' minds malleable and open to change. It was an opportunity for them to remove limiting beliefs and set some exciting new goals.

MEET THE COACHES

Each participant was assigned a coach who they would then work with for the next ninety days. Our coaches were unusual. We found coaches who had been there and done it. So when the MD of a rapidly growing company needed a coach we teamed him up with the former European Finance Director of Nike. When a new technology business sent two of their bright middle managers onto the programme we arranged for a media expert who'd built and sold a TV channel to be their coach.

TRIANGULATION

Some chief execs were worried about enrolling their staff onto our programme, fearing that after the ninety days of growth, learning and development they'd leave the organisation or undermine their boss. By ensuring the first coaching session involved the participant, the sponsor (boss) and the coach, we prevented this. We ensured the coach understood the bigger picture of the company: what the boss wanted and what the participant needed.

COACHING

Participants would then be introduced to their coaches and meet on a regular basis over the next ninety days. During these sessions our coaches could be very direct. They all knew how to coach but at times I felt some lacked a modicum of emotional intelligence and had to be challenged. Coaches need to be challenged too.

Our offices had several training rooms where many of the participants met with their coaches. I particularly enjoyed meeting with the participants before and after their coaching sessions. Some were anxious about them, but observing their journeys was amazing. It would often only take a couple of good sessions for the participant to see massive changes.

We were very fortunate to have access to such a talented coaching team and were often asked how we found them. The truth is that great coaches are everywhere and many are just waiting to be asked for their help.

SPECIALIST WORKSHOPS

Dispersed over the ninety days we also ran several workshops, which included Leadership Techniques, Advanced Communication, Time Management, and Public Speaking. As the group gelled, we would stretch them further in each of these sessions.

GRADUATION AND THE TRADING FLOOR

The last day of the programme involved a graduation event where sponsors were invited to hear the participants' reflection on the programme. We also made the event a commercial opportunity by running a trading floor activity where business transactions between the participants and their contacts were set up.

It was extraordinary to think that a group of forty people who had been together for ninety days hadn't actually done much business or helped each other until we gave them a framework to trade. But once they did – wow, on one occasion a participant did a million-pound deal there and then on the day.

The reason I'm sharing this with you is that I would imagine you either employ, work with or know some talented people right now who, with the right attention, training and a push, could become brilliant.

Edge-It

Why not create a talent programme for your brightest and best? Do it now before they decide to look for it somewhere else.

I was once pitching for a piece of work with a company that had some talented staff but unfortunately, due to poor management, lacked direction and ultimately faced all sorts of problems as a result. I was talking to the CEO about training them, and we almost had a deal when he said, 'But what if we train them and they leave?'

I had to use the cliché, 'But what if you don't and they stay?'

He thought about it for another two or three seconds, and commissioned the work.

He knew that you must have great people in your leadership pipeline. Succession planning is something Edgers are working on every day. In the long run it's less costly, less disruptive and, without a doubt, the right thing to do.

Edge-It

Succession planning is something
Edgers are working on every day.

17

The Leader's Edge

Writing this chapter is like going to a Bruce Springsteen concert: you never know when it's going to end. There's just so much to cover that I've made a decision to choose a few specific areas of leadership practised brilliantly by Edgers. Great leadership and having the

Edge go hand in hand. It's not always the case that Edgers naturally lead, but it is always the case that great leaders have the Edge.

There are thousands of books on leadership and just as many theories on leadership style. You can attend a three-day residential course to assess your leadership style and return to your workplace announcing that you're a 'blue thruster monkey' with 'purple tap-dancer inclinations'. Using this new-found knowledge, you'll explain why it's not your fault that the 'pink welder chickens' of the office don't get you. I'm kidding. Most of the leadership 'type indicators' are great and really interesting, it's just the leaders with the Edge aren't talking about them. However, I want to make several observations on the way leaders with the Edge behave that stand out.

John Elliott is a leader with the Edge. He built his company, Ebac, over forty years and then . . . gave it away. And Ebac is no small business: a conservative estimate values it at £30 million. He could have sold it, he could have given it to his daughters (who work for the company alongside John's wife Margaret), he could have stripped the assets, moved manufacturing to China and made a fortune for himself. But he didn't. Instead he handed it all over to a foundation after securing the promise that it would never sell the business or move it from the local area and that it would reinvest the profits.

More than anything, John wanted to guarantee that the 200-plus local staff would continue to be employed, and he realised that giving his business away was the best way to ensure this.

7

Edge-It
Could you give your £30 million company away?

It's not the first time John has done something on this scale. He was the first ever *Secret Millionaire* on Channel 4. When I was a fundraiser, John gave me my largest donation. And he's helped dozens of charities and local organisations too. I'm not writing this to big-up John; he'd hate that, and as I know he reads my books I'd be found out. I'm writing it because his act of selflessness typifies what brilliant leadership is all about for the Edger. Selflessness.

When Edgers are leaders they put their followers first. That last sentence sounds like the simplest, most logical way for anyone to lead, but most leaders struggle with getting the basics of selfless leadership right.

Here are the key qualities of leaders with the Edge:

AWARENESS

A heads-up meerkat approach to finding and developing people is at the forefront of the leader with the Edge. They are constantly seeking out talent and then looking for ways to develop that talent. Whether it's finding a project that will stretch them, making connections with people they could inspire or be inspired by, or letting them have enough freedom to take risks and learn from them, Edgers have an awareness of what's right.

VISION

Leaders decide where to go; managers decide how to get there. Creating a vision for an organisation and communicating it in such a way that everyone understands and buys into it is one of the most unique talents of the Edger in leadership.

When Steve Walker was selected as Chief Executive Officer for AmicusHorizon they were a failing housing association based in the south-east of England. In 2009 Steve shared a vision which he spelled out and repeated until the whole organisation got it. They wanted to be a *Sunday Times* Top 100 Company to Work For; be given the highest possible rating for an external inspection; and have the highest KPIs (key performance indicators) for any organisation in their area. His goal was to achieve all of that in just three years. To give you an idea of the scale of this challenge, if you could have put a bet on them achieving this you would have been given odds of around ten thousand to one – a real mission impossible.

However, because everyone understood the vision and understood their part in it, it quickly became a part of every meeting, every decision and every interaction. In fact, the vision became their culture.

Edge-It

When an organisation's vision and culture merge they can achieve anything.

In 2012 AmicusHorizon went straight in at No. 9 on the Best Companies To Work For listing (on their first attempt); were rated with the highest scores on external inspection (including winning a host of awards such as Investors in People Gold Standard and European Small Contact Centre of the Year); and, as I write, they are tantalisingly close to having the highest KPIs in their area – I've no doubt at all they will do it.

LISTENING

Edgers are better listeners than others, because as well as listening to what's being said they listen out for what's not being said. They have the ability to turn a simple interaction into a key moment by being more attentive and being in the zone. Sometimes the person they are communicating with isn't openly saying they have a problem. The Edger hears that. They aren't openly saying they can't do something. The Edger knows that. They don't say what's wrong because they want their leader to be happy. The Edger feels that. Edgers listen with their gut as much as they listen with their ears.

PERSUASION

Have you ever had a boss that you would gladly do anything for? Have you ever gritted your teeth and agreed to a task because your boss asked you to do it and what he/she says goes? Great leaders have the ability to persuade people to do anything for them, but with a balanced level of challenge and charisma.

The beauty is in the clarity and directness with which the

Edger gives the instruction. It's not abrupt or rude but it is clear and easily understood. Back this up with strong vision and transparent values and you'll persuade without pushing every time.

RESOURCEFUL

Have you ever played Scrabble? Christine and I play it a lot; it's good for thinking, vocabulary and strategy. So what do you believe is the number one reason when I win? Yes, that's right: it's my skill, intelligence and brilliant gamesmanship. And what do you think is the number one reason I lose? That's right: bad letters. If I just had better letters, more vowels or a 'U' to go with that 'Q' then I'd be sure to win.

Sound familiar? I've heard leaders complain that if only they had a better team they would be able to do so much more. The truth is, great leaders get the very best out of every member of their team. They'll use a person's hobbies as a resource, they'll turn a part-time position into a super-productive post, and they'll seek and develop talent in some of the most unlikely places. They'll use the experience of the old and the enthusiasm of the young.

Leaders with the Edge don't complain about their teams, even when they've inherited them. The responsibility of what they do with their team is theirs, end of. In Scrabble you have the option of passing your turn or changing all or some of your tiles.

Edge-It

The best Scrabble champions rarely trade tiles; they work to get the very best result from what they have, while planning what they'll do next. Great leaders follow this pattern with their best resources too.

INTELLECT

My friend Dilip Mukerjea wrote a book with one of the greatest titles ever: *Surfing the Intellect.* I bet you wish you'd thought of that one. People often mistake intellect for knowledge. I'd argue that intellect is what you do with knowledge. No matter how much knowledge a person has, it increases by the power of ten with the application of intellect. Leaders with the Edge understand this, so they ask better questions, allow their minds to wander, open their brains to unexplored possibilities and, most importantly, continue to be inquisitive even when they appear to know everything.

EMOTIONAL INTELLIGENCE

Being able to really understand and manage your own emotions is a skill. To understand the emotions of others is invaluable. And leaders with the Edge take this one step further, being able to perceive and utilise emotions to encourage others to deliver more than they ever thought possible. Noticing the difference between a member of your team who is bored rather than disinterested, a person who is regretful rather than ashamed, is a real talent. When that talent is properly applied, a leader can develop empathy with anyone. They understand exactly what will motivate and inspire, and their teams stick with them through thick and thin.

MORAL COMPASS

As well as doing the right thing, leaders with the Edge do things right. I'm assuming everyone has a moral compass. Following it and using it as a leader can be tough but leaders with the Edge hold this at the very heart of everything they do.

Edge-It

Imagine that your moral compass is pointing North but the wind is blowing South. What do you do?

EMPATHY

Empathy: the step beyond sympathy and a trait that most Edgers have lots of. The ability truly to empathise with another human being – to feel their pain, create an emotional connection and really understand them – sets great leaders apart from good leaders.

INSPIRING

If I were to ask you right now who you could choose to be your boss for the next twelve months, who springs to mind? I doubt it would be Dull Dave from Data Services. Most people want a boss who inspires them, who sets goals that stretch them, who encourages them and supports them to be better. If you're not a boss, can you be a leader? For the answer consider this simple question: do you inspire those around you?

STEWARDSHIP

Edgers make the most of their resources. I grew up in a house opposite a Methodist church in a village called Delves Lane. The church had six church stewards whose job it was to make sure that the building didn't fall down, that the church had the right resources (from hymn books to the heating system) and that everything was serviced regularly and properly maintained. The stewards took their role seriously, regularly arranging working parties, clearing the grounds and even building an extension. The point is, they cared about something that wasn't theirs.

Edge-It

How's your stewardship? How well do you look after company resources, people's time, client's money, family commitments, your environment and a host of other opportunities that are your responsibility?

EQUAL

Rather than needing to take the lead, Edgers are happy to share. They create outstanding partnerships where both sides feel happy about the association. These symbiotic relationships last for years. Compare this to the alpha-male relationships where leaders believe they have to be at the forefront, have to win regardless and have to be the best.

TEACHER

Finally, leaders with the Edge are happy to share and teach others what they know. They don't want to hang on to their knowledge. Nothing makes a leader with the Edge happier than finding someone who wants to learn, teaching them how to do something and seeing them take that knowledge and run with it.

Edge-It

Edgers love to give things away – especially their knowledge.

So that's my list. I'm sure you could add a dozen more. How many of those qualities, from my list and yours, do you practise? If you could only choose one to master in the next ninety days, which would it be? Well, what are you waiting for? Get on with it.

18

Magic without Misdirection

In the 1990s I was a member of the Newcastle upon Tyne Magic Circle. Often, people would ask me what you have to do to join. The answer was, 'A fifteen-minute audition and a unanimous "yes" from the committee.' You'd then pay your fee and, in return, receive a burgundy membership tie. Of course no one

joined for the tie; we wanted the secrets, the know-how, the tricks of the trade.

The best part of membership for me was the lectures. These were special events where renowned magicians would do their set and then teach you how they did it. At the end of the night they would offer an unbelievable deal to buy their lecture notes and bundles of tricks.

I was a sucker for buying everything I could get my hands on. I believed all I had to do was buy the tricks, learn the routines and then I would be as good as the lecturers. The truth, however, was entirely different.

In reality I would buy the tricks, dive straight into the pack without properly reading the instructions, get very frustrated, eventually go back to the instructions and learn the basics as quickly as possible, and then unleash my new mystic mastery on reluctant family and friends. The reaction was mixed, ranging from those who would placate me by saying 'Wow' and 'Ooh' at all the right times, to Christine, my wife and fiercest critic, who would usually ask, 'How much did you pay for that?', quickly followed by, 'You were robbed.'

After a year of membership, I agreed to help out some friends by performing at their children's parties and I'd do the odd card trick at the pub. I thought I was quite the entertainer until I went to a lecture given by a magician called Michael Ammar.

Michael Ammar did a couple of great tricks, then spent two hours explaining the psychology behind his routine: why it worked, what made it truly magical and, most importantly, what the audience were feeling at every stage of his act. He hated the thought that his audience were being fooled; he wanted them to be amazed. He frequently said his routines were less to do with misdirection and more about entertainment.

After the lecture I asked him for one piece of advice that would help me to be as good as him. He asked me how often I performed to the public, to which I answered around once a month or so. He simply replied, 'Perform public magic more often.'

Edge-It

How do you become better at performing magic in public? Simple. Perform more magic in public.

I bought his book, but this time skipped past the tricks and read about the Art of Magic. And I made a commitment: I would perform for a minimum of four hours every week. As a professional fundraiser for a children's health charity I was often asked to take part in school assemblies, speak at local Women's Institutes (and every other group or club you could imagine) and give a short address at various cheque presentations. So I had my captive audience. I included magic routines into my day job.

Although it was tough, this was the boot camp I needed to learn my craft. It became less about the tricks and more about the audience. Learning how to perform to deaf grannies and bewildered three-year-olds simultaneously earned me my stripes.

It also gave me a different insight into what gives someone

the Edge. It's more about what they know but don't do than about trying to do everything. They have an uncanny ability to create magic out of anything. These habits, once learned, are totally transferable, whether to manufacturing, hospitality, healthcare or IT.

I kept going back to my Michael Ammar book to re-read his performance notes, further understand how to sell yourself as a magician (he was very good at the business of magic too) and then delve deeper into the psychology of magic. I won some competitions and even considered turning professional.

Now, I look back on that time with great fondness, because at that time in my life everything I was learning could be applied quickly and got rapid results.

Interviewing and studying people with the Edge has shown me that they are all magicians, but not in the sense that they use misdirection or gimmicks.

Edge-It

When Edgers perform, **others** feel magic.

Here's how they do it, with some magical metaphors thrown in.

PRACTISE

Malcolm Gladwell talks about us needing to do something for 10,000 hours to become an expert. That's about three years working on something for ten hours per day. Great magicians, actors, leaders, performers, etc. have put in the hours. What do you need to work on? Where do you need to focus your 10,000 hours? How will you know when you're good enough?

USE OF PROPS

Often magicians use props that are so good they don't look like props. I paid £30 for a special £1 coin that was so well made you could inspect it and it looked just like a legitimate £1 coin. In fact it was so perfect that I didn't notice when I accidentally put it into the church collection one Sunday morning. I'm not sure which was worse: accidentally donating the coin or discovering I'd lost it halfway through a routine.

Edgers use props all the time, from prompts (you'll be surprised how many well-known singers and performers use autocue) to image enhancement, time-management technology to gizmos that make travel more productive. Here's the beauty of a great prop. You don't even know it's a prop. Edgers manage to gracefully build their use of props into their lives.

Edge-It
The right props are often used but rarely seen.

MIND READING

Magicians can't really read minds; they use tricks, devices and clever manipulation to get the 'punter' to believe their minds have been read. But maybe Edgers can? Maybe Edgers have the ability to look deep into a person's mind and uncover their hidden thoughts.

You can do this too. It involves asking the right questions, being aware of reactions and being prepared to leave your script and go 'off piste'.

Edgers notice what others don't. There's a story of Bill Gates negotiating with IBM over the use of the operating system DOS. After two days of going back and forth, late one Friday afternoon Bill Gates had a breakthrough. He knew he was going to win the negotiation the minute the IBM executives started to check their watches. It was 4.45 p.m.; Gates would have sat there all weekend.

All performers, particularly magicians and comedians, know how to read an audience. They know how far to push them, when enough really is enough and when to go for the big finish.

CLOSE-UP

Magicians love to perform close-up magic. It's intimate, personal and, when it's performed at its best, the magician finds ways for the magic to take place in the hands of the spectator. It makes the spectator the star and they 'feel' the magic. Edgers do the same. They make other people feel they are special and that they are making the magic happen. A conjuror who sets out to take the glory will often be the one who takes the fall.

Edge-It

Great close-up magicians rarely take the ovation, preferring instead to ask for applause for their volunteer.

PERFORMANCE

Great magicians are all about performing – Edgers are too. No matter how they feel, what's happening in their personal lives or whatever else is going on for them, they strive to provide a quality performance. Beatrice Tollman is the founder of Red Carnation Hotels. She's often found enthusing to her staff that working in hospitality is a performance and saying, 'You're on stage so go for it – perform.'

LEAVE THEM WANTING MORE

Magicians and Edgers will always leave you wanting more . . .

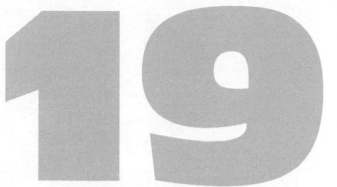

19

What 'Yes' Costs

Edgers value their time above any other resource. However, they also have different beliefs about time and how to prioritise it. Most of the people I was fortunate enough to be introduced to while researching this book were really busy people with lots of commitments. On one occasion I booked

an interview two months in the future – there's a clue there.

One of the traits that really stood out was that so many Edgers manage to complete inordinate amounts of work. They have the same twenty-four hours a day that we are all given, yet they achieve so much more and with ease. Of course there are always exceptions, mainly in the arts and creative sectors, where chaos reigned!

HOW MUCH 'YES' REALLY COSTS

Do you know how much it costs you every time you say yes? It's naïve to believe you will miss out on an opportunity or appear to be rude unless you say 'yes'. Edgers know the potential cost of 'yes' so they use the word sparingly.

Here's a scenario. You're busy, you've got a lot on and you're asked to add something else to your list. You can't drop any of the other work responsibilities you have, so what gives? Family? Health? Friends? Recovery time? Something has to go, so you give a little less time to your family – which causes some resentment, but you can handle it. On top of this, your regular work takes a slight hit, but that's OK, you'll catch up – eventually. A couple of days in and you realise you've forgotten to follow up on something. You don't relate this to the 'yes' commitment you made earlier but you're in a bit of a grump when you get home. You don't mean it to happen, but there's an air of negativity around you. Your nearest and dearest asks if you've been able to do that thing they've been talking to you about for over a week now. Boom! The fuse goes and you let them have it. 'Have you any idea how much I have on at the moment? I'm up to here, so NO, I haven't done it, and would you just get off my back!'

Do you think you may have just got your 'yes' and 'no' mixed up?

Edgers say 'yes' to family and 'no' to random opportunities. It doesn't mean you don't take opportunities but it means you are selective about which opportunities you explore. For some ideas on what's really important see Chapter 4: 'Values for Life'.

How many different products do you think Apple make? I'm going to have a look at their website now and tell you how many they focus on (PS: it's March 2012) . . . I'm back. It took me only thirty seconds because the answer is six. Yes, there are variations but generally they focus on just six products. Here's a question for you. How many different products *could* Apple make? Do you think the people at Apple know how to say 'no' often?

Those with the Edge have a brilliant ability to prioritise. They don't need complex formulas, graphs or systems. They just know what to prioritise their time on every day. I, on the other hand, do need models and methods to help me. I've several that work well but the one I couldn't function without is simple yet brilliant.

Edge-It

At the end of each day I write down the five most important things I must do tomorrow. Then I do them. And that's it.

But don't be deceived by its simplicity. It's not a 'to do' list. It's a 'Must Do' list. Notice it's not a list of everything I need to do; it's the FIVE most important things. It's not written at the start of the day when there are a dozen other distractions; it's created at the end of the day when the brain can digest and work on solutions while you sleep. And because there are just five things, decision making is easy. I can ask myself, 'Is this distraction part of my five most important things?' Yes = do it. No = ditch it.

Simple but very, very effective.

One of the other great skills of the Edger is the ability to delegate. Several of the people I studied for this book started their professional careers with tiny businesses, then grew them into huge organisations with thousands of staff. Some are high performers from entertainment, sport and the arts. All of the very best have mastered delegation.

Edge-It

Imagine delegating everything other than the stuff you really enjoy doing and the stuff you really excel at? Now that's a goal.

I asked my daughter for her thoughts on time management and delegation (it's always interesting asking a nineteen-year-old anything) and she came up with a couple of brilliant opinions. First, she likened making decisions in life to going through your post. Imagine you received six items through your door: two of them were bills, one was a subscription magazine, one was a brightly coloured envelope announcing you'd won £5,000 (*but only if you take action now!*), one was a recorded-delivery package, the final one was a beautifully hand-written envelope with a live stamp (that's a real one that you stick) and a return to sender address which you recognise and haven't heard from in ages. Which would you open first and why? Which wouldn't you open at all? If you could only open one now and the rest had to wait until tomorrow or next week, which would you choose?

This simple metaphor helps you to understand whether you make decisions based on emotion, urgency, importance or greed. This book isn't a Sunday magazine, so you won't find the answers at the back; just take a moment to consider the drivers you use to prioritise your time.

Concerning delegation, my daughter suggested that the reason most people won't let go is that we all quite like the significance or glory of doing a task. It then covers your two potential outcomes: the jobs you don't want to do but are qualified for and the jobs you do want to do but aren't qualified for. She went on to explain, 'I hate putting the rubbish out, so I'd be pleased to delegate that. However, I love the idea of flying a plane but I bet my fellow passengers are relieved that I have delegated that one.' After our little chat I felt a grid coming on.

The grid says it all.

LOW DESIRE AND LOW ABILITY

Simple, get rid of it. Do whatever it takes to delegate as much as you can in that area. There's loads of information out there on how to delegate, so I won't go into it here; what I will say is that the ability to delegate effectively was a common trait of every Edger we met.

HIGH DESIRE AND HIGH ABILITY

Do it yourself. Why not? In the majority of cases it's best for you to do the tasks that you find easy and enjoyable.

Now it gets a little more interesting.

HIGH ABILITY BUT LOW DESIRE

This is where you'll want to delegate but you must invest some time teaching the person or people you are delegating to exactly how you want it done. Treat this as a time *investment*, not time wasted. Yes it can be frustrating, yes it would be quicker if you just did it yourself, but you must get rid of these low-desirability tasks and move on to more of the high-desire activity.

FINALLY, HIGH DESIRE BUT LOW ABILITY

Again, a time investment is needed but on this occasion you become the student. Learn as much as you can about the task. Not necessarily so that you'll do it all yourself, but to give you scope and choice about what you do with it later. For the last few years many of my major projects have involved making videos. Initially I would use a production crew to do everything. I wasn't that interested in the filming side but I loved to see how the editing was done. The challenge was I could never justify spending my time editing my own videos as I (a) didn't have the skill and (b) didn't have the time.

I recently evaluated this and signed up to one-to-one training on how to professionally edit videos. Now I am able to edit my own films and, even if I don't have the time to do the edit, I'm much better at briefing an editor and would be able to take over a project midway. But the best bit is – I love it!

Edge-It

Edgers make time to manage their time.

Time doesn't just happen for Edgers; they don't run out of it and they certainly don't waste it. You can read dozens of books on how to manage your time. I've written one which guarantees to *save you an hour every day*, but unless you start with the mindset that you can manage your time, you can be sure that time will manage you.

20

Don't Take Anything for Granted

E dgers question everything.

It's not that they doubt what you say; it's more a case of needing to know. Because Edgers thrive on information, they will constantly question data, information, a person, everything.

My friend Alex has the Edge. A few years ago he and his wife Anne sold their business. It was time to slow down and relax. The problem was that after six weeks Alex got bored and started to search for a new challenge. Even though his background had been in chemist's shops and pharmacy supplies he ended up buying a glass company. On his first day he walked the factory floor talking to the staff and asking them questions. He wanted to know what they did, what they needed and their ideas on how things could be improved. The next day he did the same journey and talked to the same people again. On Wednesday he took his third walk around the factory floor. While he was talking to one of the manufacturing team, asking him questions about how the week was going, etc., the chap he was talking to suddenly said, 'Hang on. What's this all about?'

Alex was slightly taken aback.

'Well, you've been here for three days and in that time you've talked to me and asked me more questions than the old boss did in a year!'

It's no surprise that Alex has turned that business around. It's gone from making a loss to being highly profitable in a few months. At the core of the turnaround was the need to question everything.

Edge-It

Questioning isn't about finding out what's wrong – it's about an enquiry to make things better.

The questioning mind of the Edger can sometimes be an irritation to those around them. They want to know every detail because of the desire to make things better, so the more astute Edger depends on a level of tact and diplomacy.

I'm sure you've been in the situation where you're on the receiving end of an enquiry that feels more like an interrogation. You become defensive and give the minimum amount of information. You begin to wonder what's behind the questions and the wedge of doubt is hammered home. Then there are other times when you've received an enquiry and felt comfortable with the questions. You're happy to give information and offer additional insight.

So why is it that one person can make you feel informed and invaluable while another makes you feel goaded and grilled?

For the Edger it's all about intent. By starting out with the right intention you're always going to get the best out of an enquiry. Let's go back to Alex. When he took on the glass company his primary goal was to create a great glass company. The profit would be the by-product of creating a successful business. Alex is also passionate about people. He genuinely wants to know what makes them tick so he can understand their motivation.

Now let's imagine a different Alex. This Alex is only interested in turning a profit and his primary goal is to run the factory to the max and cut costs. He wants to know what everyone does so that he can either give them more work or get rid of them. How might he come across?

Here are five questions to consider before every enquiry:

1. What do I really need to know? Need to know and want to know are two different things. Sometimes our desire to be nosey gets in the way of carefully finding the information we require.

2. What's in it for the person I'm asking? Great enquiry is a dialogue. What can you give them? Find out what they want and, if possible, give it to them as soon as you can.
3. Listen. And by listen I mean REALLY listen. We're all guilty at times of thinking more about the next thing we will say rather than listening to what's being said.
4. Make follow-up questions about the person who is giving the information rather than about the information on its own. For example, rather than simply asking 'Why?' ask, 'Why would you do that?', 'What would you do?', 'How would you do . . . ?', etc.
5. Know when to stop. If you take too many withdrawals don't be surprised when you go overdrawn. Edgers know when to shut up and move on and, importantly, when to leave an enquiry altogether.

Edge-It

Questioning others is great; you'll learn a lot and quickly. However, Edgers are great at questioning themselves too.

When most people question themselves they associate the practice with creating doubt. Edgers question themselves to create confidence. It's another instance where a slight adaptation gets outstanding results.

A selection of questions that some of the Edgers we interviewed ask themselves when they want to make things better are:

Does this need to be done? I love this question. It's a fundamental of time management as it's usually followed with, 'If so, do I need to do this?' and completed with, 'If not, who can do it for me?'

Why? A why usually leads to another why and is generally followed by many more. Edgers are usually asking why because they want to simplify their lives, not further complicate them. Their ability to peel back the onion skin to get to the core of an issue often starts with the question, 'Why?'

What does this really mean? It's not that Edgers doubt the information they are given, it's just that their intuition says there's more to this than meets the eye. By asking 'softer' questions around meaning rather than looking for direct answers, Edgers uncover some remarkable truths.

What would make this even better? It's not that Edgers don't appreciate what's available here and now, it's just a desire to improve, well . . . everything!

Who should be involved? Because they have a network of people they can tap into, Edgers are constantly asking who needs to be involved with a project, decision, etc. to make it better.

For more questions Edgers ask themselves go to Chapter 8: 'Asking Great Questions'.

The ability to ask great questions and have an enquiring mind is a gift. The real gift is being able to control the amount of questioning you do. Edgers know when to turn it on and, most importantly, when to turn it off.

21

Decision Making on the Edge

One of the key qualities of those with the Edge is their ability to make decisions. Even if they make the wrong decision it doesn't matter so long as they decide to do something. And it's that ability to decide and take action that sets them apart.

Edge-It

When it comes to decision making, it's the ability to decide and take action that sets Edgers apart.

For many people, making decisions is a painful task. They'd rather think about it, come back to it when . . . or they feel they need more information. Those with the Edge don't (on the surface) appear to need that. However, when you dig deeper into their decision-making process, although swift it usually involves some kind of routine. The key factors are rapidly considered and if all of these factors line up then a decision is made. And because those with the Edge have the ability to consider key factors at speed, their decision-making process appears to be effortless.

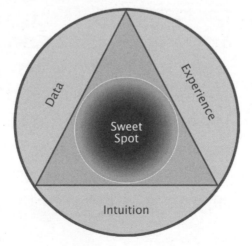

The good news for the rest of us is that we can learn how to use that same process to help our decision making.

The factors are **data**, **experience** and **intuition**.

When all three line up, the sweet spot of rapid decision making is achieved.

DATA

Superficially, data would appear to be the easiest of the three to influence. However, too much data can slow down the decision-making process.

Analysis Paralysis

This is when you attempt to take in and consider too much information, your belief being that a decision can't be made until you have all the data to form your opinion. The challenge is, you will never have all the data. Those with the Edge know this and also know that you don't need all the data – just the correct data. They set up their decision-making model to ensure they only get the information they require, at the right time and presented in the right way.

You can do this too by asking yourself three simple questions about the data that is streaming into your life.

1. Do I need this? If the answer is no, switch off that tap.
2. Is this enough? If the answer is no, ask for more. It's amazing what people will make available to you – if you only ask.

3. What will make this data better? Is it the presentation? Is the data source a challenge? If you need to, challenge the data and challenge the source.

EXPERIENCE

'I don't have the experience!' That's a wimp's way of not making a decision. Great decision makers remove this excuse by using a brilliant 80 per cent rule. Their thinking goes along the lines of, 'Is this situation similar to other experiences I have had in the past?' If there's an 80 per cent match then you're in business.

I used to run an events management company. In the early stages of the business we were given the opportunity to bid for a job to stage a conference for 2,500 delegates. Until that point we had only organised events for up to 200. One of my team advised caution, suggesting it would be ten times as complex. Rubbish! I knew 80 per cent of the work was exactly the same as we had experienced and successfully carried out in the past. We knew how to do that brilliantly so 2,500 would be easy. Well I was half right – we could do it, but I'd be fibbing if I said it was easy. However, once we had one large-scale conference under our belt it quickly became apparent that we could do large events. From that moment, audience numbers were never an issue.

The following Edge-It may encourage you to worry less about having all the experience you may think you need to make decisions.

Edge-It

Lack of experience can lead to bad decisions.
Bad decisions usually lead to more experience.
More experience leads to better decisions.
Better decisions lead to greater success.

INTUITION

I'm going to write more on this factor than on the other two combined. You'll know how much I love intuition from Chapter 1; well, there's even more in this chapter, because intuition is brilliant. It's always right. Even when you think it's wrong, it invariably turns out to be right! The challenge you face isn't that you don't have good intuition, it's that you don't know how to listen to it.

Edgers know how to tune in to their intuition and how to use it to help them make rapid, accurate decisions.

The interesting thing about your intuition is that you are only aware of it when something goes wrong and you didn't listen to it. 'I knew I should have said no.' 'I could have done that so much better if I'd called rather than emailed.' 'I've missed my opportunity; I wish I'd been more proactive when I had the chance.' I'm sure you'll recognise that type of scenario.

When you do listen to your intuition and things turn out well (as they invariably do when you listen to and use your intuition) you'll rarely put your success down to your intuitive nature. You're just grateful that everything turned out well.

The first step to developing a better intuition is to be aware of when you've used it and what you achieved, whether in relation to small almost trivial things through to major life-changing decisions. As an exercise for the next twenty-four hours, ask your intuitive self lots of small questions. 'Should I have tea or coffee?' 'Should I watch this TV show or read a book?' 'Should I go out with my friends or stay in?' Ask the questions and listen for your intuitive voice. It's there and it's giving you quick decisive answers.

For the next seven days avoid the phrase, 'I don't know.' You do know! Just ask your intuitive self and then listen. It may be that you get a simple 'yes' or 'no', or it may feel like a hunch. Either way, go with whatever your intuition tells you. Every few hours take a couple of minutes to think about the intuitive decisions you have made and the results of those decisions. This type of mental training is brilliant for developing your insight and decision-making skills.

Edge-It

You'll quickly realise your intuition is making all the right decisions.

Another way to develop your intuition is to ask 'What if' questions. I'm sure you're familiar with this simple concept, often used in brain-storming sessions. 'What if money was no object?', 'What if we did it ten times faster?', 'What if we moved it to China?'.

This straightforward question can be used to help to develop your intuition. And it doesn't need to be wild brain-storming 'What if's', just simple questions such as: 'What if we waited one week?' 'What if we made it 10 per cent cheaper?' 'What if I skipped lunch and went to the gym?' The important part of this process is to listen to what your intuition says immediately after the question has been asked.

For many years Michael Ray, PhD, has taught Personal Creativity in Business as part of Stanford University's MBA pro-gramme. He talks about there being five truths of intuition. These are the truths that many business people find difficult to accept; however, if they do accept them and live by these truths they can develop their intuition remarkably in business and life. They are:

1. Intuition must be developed. Each of us has intuition within us, but we must accept the responsibility for our individual style of intuition and its development.
2. Intuition and reason are complements. It is the combination of reason, experience, information and intuition that is so powerful.
3. Intuition is unemotional. It is paying attention clearly to the most appropriate alternative that comes from the creative essence.
4. Intuition requires action. Follow-through is key to successful use of intuition in business. It requires timely hard work.
5. Intuition is mistake free. There will always be

'rational' reasons to support intuitive leaps. Beyond this we must have absolute faith that the intuitive part of us does not make mistakes.

My favourite in this list is number five. *Intuition is mistake free.* I love it! I really feel developing intuition for decision making is easier than you think. Play with 'What if' scenarios, consider the options you're presented with and take action.

Think about how much faster your decision making could be if you knew how to tap into your intuition? Edgers feel more comfortable making decisions because they make more of them. They know that once a decision is made, they can, if they need to, adjust it (sometimes), change their mind (rarely), and, most importantly, move forward.

The next time you find yourself procrastinating instead of making a decision, stop. Then look deep into your intuition and follow your gut. What do you feel is right? Once you've got it, make a decision and act on it. On the rare occasion when you make a decision that could have been better just learn from it and let it go. At least you made a decision.

Compare this with the paralysis of inactivity: never knowing what would happen, fearing making the wrong decision, so doing nothing.

Edge-It

The more you test your intuition the easier it gets. Edgers use it so much their intuition comes naturally.

BRINGING IT ALL TOGETHER

The most important rule the Edgers live by is that *they* will make the decision. It may not always be perfect. The ability to make rapid decisions puts them in a minority. Nonetheless, such people are respected, trusted and considered the leaders.

Making decisions quickly and effectively is one of the key characteristics of those who have the Edge. My challenge to you is take action and put your decision making to the test. Will you do it? And will you do it now?

22

How to
be a
Super
Speaker

One of the greatest character-istics of people who have the Edge is their ability to speak in public. Whether it's on a main stage, during meetings or in a small group, they can take any presentation and turn it into something very special.

Have you ever sat in the audience at a large conference featuring many speakers? The one with the Edge is able to stand on stage and address thousands of people and every single one of them is focused on that person. You can't hear a cough, sniff, sneeze or shuffle. However, someone who has just as important a message to deliver but doesn't have the Edge has to work hard to get the audience's initial attention. Then they have to work even harder to hold the audience's attention. The content of both presentations could have been identical but whose is remembered? Who do people refer back to? Who gets the opportunities when others are left behind?

Edge-It

Great speakers get the opportunities that average (or non-)speakers don't. They are the ones who are remembered when others are quickly forgotten.

When someone is able to communicate in such a way that an audience feels inspired, engaged and ready to take action that's when the speaker has the Edge. And the good news is, there are certain characteristics of these great communicators that anyone can learn.

It's not about the size of the audience or the platform. Pitching an idea to three colleagues at a weekly update meeting can be as important as presenting the five-year plan at your annual conference. The principles remain the same and when you've got them you'll go from loathing the idea of presenting to loving it.

I'm very fortunate that I've had the opportunity to present to over half a million people around the world and share a stage with some very well-known presenters. Every time I meet one of those people I ask them, 'How do you do it?'

Usually they respond with a quizzical look and ask what I mean. I explain that I want to know what it is they are mentally and physically doing before, during and after a presentation. I especially want to know how they are feeling when they are presenting and when they are in their 'zone'.

Interestingly, their responses indicate that what gives them the Edge is less about natural confidence and more about the tools and techniques they use. Over the years I've distilled this information and tested dozens of ideas before finding out which ones work for everyone and which are best left to the professionals.

I now teach people to present. My clients range from specialist speakers who want to improve, to terrified first-timers who want to get it over with. I believe there is a framework you can build on that will vastly improve your ability to present to any audience, large or small.

Start by answering these questions and mark where you land on the lines below:

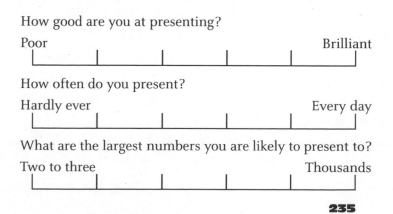

How good are you at presenting?

Poor   Brilliant

How often do you present?

Hardly ever   Every day

What are the largest numbers you are likely to present to?

Two to three   Thousands

The Edge

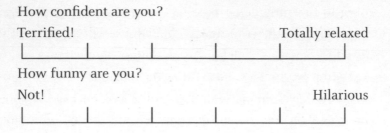

How confident are you?

Terrified!   Totally relaxed

How funny are you?

Not!   Hilarious

If you've found yourself mainly on the right-hand side then still make sure you read and do everything in this chapter to help you get the Edge and move your presenting skills to the next level. Then make sure you thoroughly digest the following chapter, where you'll learn the 'tricks of the trade'. If you find yourself mainly on the left then the good news is that if you read everything in this chapter and test the ideas, you'll soon find yourself stepping up as a presenter and actually enjoying the process. If you're mainly in the middle then you'll love these ideas and you'll get rapid results when you test them out.

This chapter features ten 'must do's' that I want you to apply to every presentation you deliver. I'm going to blow my own trumpet here. My passion isn't writing – it's presenting to live audiences. And I have to say, I'm pretty good. I've been described as one of the top three professional speakers in the world. That's quite a responsibility. It's like being described as one of the top three chefs in the world, then having to cook for a panel who are watching your every move. You have to prepare a unique signature dish – and it'd better be brilliant.

When I stand on stage I have to feel confident that I'm

going to have the Edge to deliver exactly what my audience expects from the moment I begin until long after I've closed.

My top ten must do's are the foundation for every presentation. Some need to be done way before you take to the stage, others are carried out during your performance. Remember, this isn't about getting through it, doing a half-decent job or just being a bit better. This is about presenting with the Edge to make your presentation engaging, memorable and enjoyable (for you and your audience, whatever their size).

STEP ONE: PREPARE, PREPARE, PREPARE

It starts with preparation. As boring as that may seem, preparation, preparation, preparation is the first key to great speech making.

I once had a heated discussion with a participant on my speaking course who said you could be 'too well prepared'. He told the story of how he once had to just stand up and give a presentation at a conference because his boss had been taken ill at the last minute. He didn't have any notes, slides or preparation time but he 'slayed them' (unfortunate choice of words I thought) and was the hero of the hour.

It turned out that this heroic performance had occurred four years earlier and he hadn't had anything like that level of success since. Living on a one-off past glory isn't what those who present with the Edge focus on. They're too busy creating, designing and practising what's next.

Edge-It

Brilliant presentations that happened 'off the cuff' are more likely to be down to luck. The best speakers practise and plan.

Here's a checklist to consider:

1. Who's in the audience?
2. What do they really need to know?
3. How long do I have to present?
4. Where am I presenting?
5. Do I need equipment?
6. What do I want people to do differently after my presentation?
7. Who's on before me and after me? What will they be saying?
8. When will I plan my presentation?
9. Who will be happy to listen to my run-through and give me honest feedback?

Once you've answered those questions you can start to create your masterpiece. And here's what all great presentations have in common.

STEP TWO: PLAN THE START AND THE END

Past advice was that you should present in the same way that newsreaders do as they lead you through the news. This would mean giving your audience:

A hint of what you would cover – the headlines.
The bulk of your presentation – the news.
A review of what you said – a final look at the headlines.

The problem with that method is that it's been around for ages and reflects a time when we had three TV channels and the news was something you watched twice a day. Now we've over three hundred channels and each one of them is vying for your time and attention. News has become a smarter proposition, and we need to be too.

One of the ways the news channels work to maintain interest is to create mini cliff-hangers at the start, in the trailers and especially between the ad breaks. To close these 'open loops' you have to watch to see what happens next.

Here's how you can do the same with your opening.

The old way of opening a presentation may have sounded something like this:

'This afternoon I'm going to cover the last quarter's trading, present the figures by product line with some recommendations, and give an estimation of the Q3 operating position.'

Here's how someone with the Edge might present the same piece:

'This afternoon I'm going to take you on a journey through the highs and lows of the last ninety days. I'll expose where we're making money, where we're losing money and what needs to change. And I'll finish by sticking my neck out and making a prediction that may surprise you all.'

Whose presentation would you most like to listen to?

Now let's look at closing. There is only one way to end a presentation and it's based on an assumption. The assumption being that BOTH you and your audience know you've finished. Sounds obvious, but overlooking this is a classic mistake.

Your Audience Thinks You're Closing but You're Not

Typically it goes something like this: 'And finally', or 'One more thing . . .' As soon as you make a positioning statement you have sixty seconds to wrap up and get off. A second longer and you've lost your audience.

You've Finished but Your Audience Doesn't Know That

So you haven't prepared a close or clearly indicated you've finished. The best way to show that you're all done is to hold your hands slightly out from your sides, palms facing towards your audience, and dip your head as you say 'Thank you'. This is a universal cue that the presentation, act, speech, etc., is over.

Once you've worked out the start and the end you can work on the middle.

Edge-It

Great presenters always have a well-rehearsed memorable start and a brilliant ending. Most importantly, they make sure they're not too far apart.

STEP THREE: THE MIDDLE

Find out how long you have to present, and plan your speaking time to be 25 per cent shorter, because even on a run-through you'll do it faster than when you are presenting live.

Keep asking yourself the question: 'Does this add to my key messages or is it a distraction?' If in doubt – miss it out.

I'm not going to tell you what to talk about here; it's my job to give you the Edge so I'm going to make the assumption that you know your stuff and you're going to make it interesting.

STEP FOUR: AVOID AT ALL COSTS DBPP

DBPP is causing challenges all over the world. It's taking potentially great presentations and turning them into dull yarns. DBPP is driving people nuts and with over 100 million people having access to it, it's hardly surprising that DBPP is the number one criticism from audiences about their speakers. DBPP is Death By Power Point.

Don't get me wrong, PowerPoint is a brilliant invention.

However, it was designed to enhance what the speaker is doing and not to replace it. Here are the most irritating, distracting and boring things that people do with PowerPoint:

1. Read the slides. Arrrrggggg. It's PowerPoint, not autocue. If you don't know what to say, get some cue cards. An average person can read at two hundred and fifty to three hundred words per minute. The average speed of a person presenting is around a hundred words per minute. Get it? Your audience will have read your slides three times faster than you did and now they're nodding off.
2. Too many words on a slide. This goes back to point one. It's not autocue. You only need a few words on a slide. As a rule of thumb, around twelve words max.
3. If your audience can't read it, don't put it in. I don't care how long logistics took to prepare that graph, if it isn't screaming something amazing then take it out.
4. Poor colour choices. If you're unsure, go to Dave Pardi's website thinkoutsidetheslide.com and use the 'Color Contrast Calculator'; it will tell you which colours work and what looks pretty.
5. Too much animation. Find one simple transition you like and stick with it.
6. Standing in front of the projector.
7. Not testing the equipment beforehand and setting up during the meeting while everybody watches you.

Here are a few alternatives to using PowerPoint:

- Flash cards. Boldly printed cards were considered old school but now they are right on the money.
- Props. The use of one or two carefully selected props will be more memorable than fifty 'so what' slides.
- Flip chart. Yes remember the good old flip chart? If you are going to use one, ensure it has shiny paper and use VERY fat markers.
- Video. Now easy to make, edit and play. A customer talking about their experience for thirty seconds is worth its weight in gold.

Edge-It
Avoid DBPP*

STEP FIVE: TIMING, PART 1

Before you think I'm going to share with you the secrets of comic timing or a powerful pause there are two other timings to consider. Getting there early and how long you're presenting for.

Here's what the amateurs do. You've been asked to speak at your quarterly update. You're on at 1.30 p.m., straight after lunch. You arrive at 1.15 p.m., find the bloke from AV with the

* Death By PowerPoint

computer and hand him a memory stick with your presentation on it. Although it's the wrong version of PowerPoint your operator manages to open the file – phew.

Now you want to change a couple of slides so you proceed to tell the 'techie' what you want taken out, reordered, etc., and could he just make that a bit bigger and the other thing a little smaller? You're on in seconds, struggling through an unfamiliar presentation with a strong desire to just get through it. Because you haven't timed your presentation you end up skipping through the last five slides – much to the bemusement of the audience, who are now wondering what you've missed out. The presentation doesn't go down well, so you blame the fact that the 'techie' was too slow and, anyway, you had the after-lunch graveyard slot!

The chief exec makes a mental note not to ask you to present again.

Edge-It

The 'graveyard slot' is the excuse poor speakers make when they lose their audience.

Here's how someone with the Edge would do it. You've prepped and practised your presentation. You've put the slides on a background supplied by your communications team so that it fits with that used during the rest of the day. You've sent your slides over early and have them with you on a memory stick as a back-up.

You arrive before lunch and immediately check that everything is OK with the 'techies', knowing that if you get in a fix these guys can make or break your presentation. Next you make a beeline for the communications team and ask them if there is anything you should know from the morning session that may impact on your presentation.

You take to the stage and nail it. On message and on time. Everyone comments that your information was insightful and presented with energy, and it just so happens the chief exec now has her eye on you for all the right reasons.

Edge-It

The most important rule of 'timing' is to arrive early.

STEP SIX: TIMING, PART 2

Now we can look at the more traditional form of timing using three headings: Pace, Pause and Posture.

Pace

Let's start with pace. Knowing how many words you deliver per minute is a useful tool. I deliver at around a hundred and fifty words per minute and can peak at a hundred and eighty. I know, I am a very fast speaker. However, I read at around three hundred words per minute. So if I were to write a presentation and read it back in my head I would need double the time to present it. YES, DOUBLE! This is one of the most common mistakes people make. They get a fifteen-minute slot, write what they believe is a fifteen-minute presentation and it takes them thirty minutes to present it. It's disrespectful, causes you and the event organiser's stress and professionals just don't do it.

The only way to practise a presentation is to say it out loud. Your pace should be steady and clear so that when you want to slow something down or speed it up to make a point your audience knows you've changed your stride for a reason.

> # Edge-It
> The **only** way to practise a presentation is to say it out loud.

Pause

Some of the best speakers in the world make their point by saying . . . nothing. They are able to hold a room with a silence that feels completely natural and yet in any other circumstance would be so excruciatingly uncomfortable you would be desperate to fill that noiseless gap.

The question is, how many pauses and for how long? Steve McDermott suggests you take a lead from the humble Kit Kat.

What's the strap line for a Kit Kat? 'Have a break'. It's the same when you speak. At the right times, have a break and be prepared to fill it with . . . nothing: just simple silence.

Kit Kats come in all shapes and sizes these days and you can use this to create chocolatey metaphors to help you decide how long to pause and how many pauses you need to use.

First up are Kit Kat 'Pop Chocs'. You buy them in bags, each is only about a centimetre cubed and you get forty to fifty in a pack. These represent a short one-second (count of one) pause. And, just as if you were eating the 'Pop Chocs', you can have as many as you like.

The next Kit Kats are what I call the classics. They're ones you'd find in your packed-lunch box. Two fingers of biscuity chocolatey bliss. (Was it only me or every so often did you get a Kit Kat that was more solid chocolate than crispy wafer? Yum.) Anyhow, they represent a count of two. You could eat two or three of these and that's the same number of pauses you can put into a presentation.

Finally there's the Kit Kat Chunky. It's the mother of all Kit Kats and most people are happy with just one. It's the same with your presentation: you'll only have one Kit Kat Chunky pause in it because it will last for . . . as long as it takes to get the whole audience completely focused on you.

Take the following sentences and test them out by reading them straight and then inserting the three types of pause between the two sentences. Which works best?

'I have a very special announcement that will affect everyone in this room. Next year this organisation will introduce
. . . abc'

Pop Choc – count of one
Classic – count of two
Chunky – as long at it takes

A pause is a powerful thing. If you lose your way, take a pause. If you need time to think, use a pause. If you normally err or umm, replace it with a pause.

Edge-It

Silence is the friend of confident presenters who have the Edge.

STEP SEVEN: MADE A MISTAKE? GET OVER IT!

Everyone makes mistakes. Here's a secret: most people won't know or care that you've made a mistake unless you point it out. Getting facts the wrong way round, missing a chunk out, forgetting a key piece of information are all forgivable IF you don't dwell on them.

Years ago, if a radio presenter made a mistake they would apologise for it. Now you'll rarely hear that. Mainly because you wouldn't have noticed the fact that they'd made the error until they pointed it out to you! Most people notice an apology more than a mistake. So, in simple terms, go with the majority; don't go back, just kick on with your piece.

STEP EIGHT: DON'T OVERDO IT

There's only one thing worse than someone who puts no emotion into a presentation – and that's the person who uses too much. It's like a bad opening night at your local amateur dramatics club. You've seen them, heard them and felt for them.

There is no 'off' button, no way of getting them to calm down and, worst of all, the message is usually lost in the mêlée.

Here are few simple thoughts:

- Project – don't shout.
- Use your arms – don't throw them about.
- Tone should be controlled, up and down – not up, up, up!
- If your audience is wincing, it's a signal to you. Take notice.

STEP NINE: BREATHE

I've watched brilliant speakers turn nerves into positive energy in seconds by breathing correctly for half a minute. Such is the amazing power of taking deep breaths before you speak. That's BEFORE you speak, not during (see Step eight: 'Don't overdo it').

Over the years I've tested out lots of breathing techniques but the one that works in most cases for most people is to use the 4–8–6 method. This means you breathe in through your nose for a count of four, hold it for a count of eight and exhale for a count of six.

Do this five or six times and you'll instantly feel more relaxed. You'll give your brain a burst of oxygen and you'll feel calm enough to take to the stage, but you'll still have enough oomph for your presentation.

STEP TEN: LESS IS MORE

No one wants a presentation to over-run, no matter how good your speaking is.

Edge-It

Say what you need to say. Then say thank you. Then leave.

That top ten checklist will help you to create a foundation and framework for every presentation. But this book is all about getting the Edge, and making your presentations pertinent, pacey and powerful is what makes them memorable. Turn the page for how you can take your presenting to the next level.

23

Standing Ovations - the Tricks of the Trade

One of the features of being a professional speaker is you get to see and meet other professional speakers. Even if there's a dressing room at a big event you won't find me in there. I'm either in the wings or with the audience taking notes and learning. Over the years I've built up

an arsenal of what I call the *tricks of the trade*. These are the hints and tips that really give a presenter the Edge.

And it doesn't matter if you are presenting to a handful of colleagues or at a national convention – the principles remain the same.

THE POWER OF THREE

Three really is a magic number and outstanding orators know how to use it. Remember when Tony Blair gave his 1997 pledge to put 'Education, Education, Education' at the top of his list of priorities. One less and it would have been, 'Education and Education' and that feels weak. One more and it would have been 'Education, Education, Education, Education' and that would have sounded like the record was stuck. Three was the magic number.

When I describe my job I say, 'I'm a gap filler. I find out where people are now and where they want to be. Then I help them to fill the gap; as quickly as possible, as economically as possible and with as much fun as possible.'

Now there are probably a few other things I do too, but three is the magic number. Many great speeches use the power of three. From 'Friends, Romans, countrymen . . .' in Shakespeare's *Julius Caesar* to the finale of Martin Luther King's famous 'I have a dream' speech: 'Free at last! Free at last! Thank God Almighty, we are free at last!'

A good way to test the power of three is to describe what

you do using a power of three. Think about the cadence of the words and use alliteration to enhance your message.

Edge-It

Three is the magic number.

CLOCK THEM

Most people don't know where to look when presenting. They may find a friendly face in their audience and latch on, leaving the rest of the room feeling left out. Or become laser focused on a point at the back of the room, leaving the entire audience feeling lost. Some bury their heads in notes or screens.

When I'm presenting, I imagine the room as a clock face. My job is to look at every number on the clock. I may start at one, then move to seven, jump up to nine and move over to four, etc. By doing this, the whole room will at some point get your focus. All audiences want to feel that on occasions they got the speaker's undivided attention.

Edge-It

Everyone, even in an audience of thousands, should feel like they have had eye contact with you at least once during your presentation.

EMBEDDED COMMANDS

I could write a book on this one (and others have) so I'll just whet your appetite. If you'd like to know more, you can always Google it. Using embedded commands while speaking is when the audience is given some additional information (usually something to do) as part of the presentation without the presenter actually saying it. Let me give you an example.

Imagine you are presenting some good news and some bad news about your department's performance. At the end of the presentation you want to ask for some additional resources to do something new and risky. How do you increase your chances of getting a 'yes'?

Well, let's assume you've done all your homework, have a good argument, etc. This could be the technique that tips the balance. When you talk about the good news stuff and how well you have done, 'embed' this to something inanimate. You could stand in a certain part of the room or maybe hold a blue marker pen. When you talk about the bad news embed this to something else. You may move to another part of the room (just a couple of steps is enough) or hold a red marker pen. It doesn't really matter what it is so long as your audience appreciate there is a difference.

When it comes to asking for the additional resources for your new project, stand in the 'good news' spot or hold the blue marker pen. In doing this you fire subconscious messages into the minds of the people you are presenting to. You're telling them, 'This is good news.'

It's not an exact science but I and many others have had great results using embedded commands.

Another simple way of doing this is to point at yourself when talking about success or positive outcomes. How you point is quite important here. I use both hands and point eight fingers towards my chest; it's subtle and it feels like a natural gesture. I'm sure it's better and a lot more 'embedded' than pointing one finger at the side of my head!

You can do this with words too. When you say to your audience, 'You don't have to release the resources for this project, but if you do . . .' your audience will immediately begin to focus on releasing resources. It's like when someone says, 'Don't think of elephants', and you immediately think of . . .

That's right, you even finished the sentence because the thought of elephants has been embedded.

A word of warning. If you decide to find out more about embedded commands via the internet be careful what you watch and read; some of these guys are very good and who knows what they'll drop into your mind via a YouTube video.

DOUBLE UP

If you are talking to more than twenty people, then it's time to double up your gestures, tones, emphasis, etc. It's a tipping point where you are no longer able to connect with everyone individually, so you need to be able to capture each person in the room simultaneously. You'll still use the 'Clock Them' approach, but you will also need to up your presentation so that it becomes more of a performance. You may feel a little uncomfortable with this but to the audience it's still a presentation – it's just more engaging.

> ## Edge-It
>
> For larger groups, if you would normally gesture by moving your arm eight inches, make it sixteen. If you would normally hold your hand up level with your ear, put it above your head. Vary your tone and pace in the same way.

GETTING RID OF ERRS, UMMMS AND 'YOUR THING'

Most people when they are presenting have a 'thing' they do while they are thinking or just filling a gap. The challenge is that you probably don't know what yours is.

When I first started to speak professionally I was given the opportunity to tour with a company that was launching a new product. The tour lasted for almost three weeks and I was one of two presenters who would talk for forty minutes each. Four times a day!

My job was to get the local staff for this company excited about the new product. My contemporary had to give a technical training demonstration so they would understand what the product did.

After the first morning, the other presenter complimented me on my presentations but felt the need to tell me that I had a 'thing' that I did while presenting. Always interested in improving, I asked him to tell me what 'the thing' was. It turned out that I said 'erm' a lot while speaking, usually to fill a gap. I was gutted. I didn't 'erm'; I was certain of that. So I suggested he must be mistaken. I also pointed out that his 'thing' was that he said the word 'actually' unnecessarily throughout his presentation. (I was probably feeling a little vindictive after he'd commented on my 'erm' habit.)

Of course he denied it, so we had a chat with the guys from the AV company and asked if they would record one of the afternoon sessions. That night we played it back, and he was right – I managed over sixty 'erms'; however, he had almost as many 'actuallys'.

It was kind of him to point out my 'thing' but what was more important was what we both did next. For the following three weeks, every time I said 'erm' I had to pay him £1 and every time he said 'actually' he had to pay me the same. By the end of three weeks a few thousand pounds had changed hands but I wasn't 'erm-ing' and he'd finished 'actually-ing'.

Edge-It

Find an honest Joe who will tell you what your 'thing' is. It could be how you stand, the way you say a word, how you look at the audience, a random word or an 'erm' or 'umm'. Once you've identified it, you can work on eliminating it. It's a bit clunky at first because it's a habit. But once you've changed you'll be one step closer to having the speaker's Edge.

The Edge

Finally, the very best way to present with the Edge is to present from the heart. No amount of carefully polished practice can replace a presentation that comes from the heart of a person who really cares.

24

Similes, Metaphors and Other Analogies

I love similes, metaphors and analogies and so do many Edgers.

The ability to use them effectively has always fascinated me as a presenter. They can assist in explaining any complicated scenario, system or idea.

A few years ago I was asked to coach the new chief executive of a large company, as he was due to make a speech to his whole organisation at their annual national conference. It was a big moment for him. He'd only been with the company for a few months, had immense ambition and had already started to make extensive changes to the business.

I asked him what the primary purpose was of his speech. He told me he wanted to get everyone onside and make certain they all bought into his vision for the future of the company. He ran through the outline of his presentation: what he would be saying and the slides he'd prepared. Hmmm . . . I felt he was miles off. When I'm coaching clients I often feel it's best to be as direct as possible. This was one of those occasions. So I told him what I felt the outcome would be if he continued down his proposed route.

The presentation he had planned wouldn't have inspired anyone. His vision for the future was hidden away amongst a plethora of slides featuring detailed graphs and cluttered numbers. Worse still, he hated his own presentation. We agreed to start again from scratch.

A couple of hours later his speech was reborn using a powerful metaphor. Here's how he delivered his presentation.

He began by walking on stage with a large red box which he placed on a table. Then he asked the audience if they had ever completed a jigsaw puzzle. This simple start had the whole room intrigued and brought all of their thinking together. He had the audience rapt in less than ten seconds. He then went on to explain that he always did jigsaw puzzles using the same formula. First he would find the four corners. 'I wonder how many of you do the same?' he asked. The whole room nodded.

He then went on to explain that his first few months at the company had been like putting a jigsaw puzzle together. Finding the four corners was the equivalent of establishing his top four priorities: people, products, production and price.

Next, he said, he liked to find all the edge pieces of a jigsaw. This was like determining the boundaries of the business; knowing what was or wasn't currently achievable. The whole audience was enthralled as he explained each point and what it meant for him, them and the business.

Returning to his analogy of a jigsaw, he told them how he liked to find similar pieces of the puzzle and do the easy bits first. Who doesn't?

He announced that the jigsaw wasn't complete but it was getting close. He asked the audience if they were familiar with the feeling of near completion, as when there are only a few pieces of the jigsaw left. No matter how tired you are, you'll stay up to get it finished. And that's how he felt about the business now – he wouldn't rest until all the pieces were in place.

Finally, he remarked that no one would dream of starting a jigsaw unless they knew what the finished puzzle was meant to look like. At that point he picked up the red box that he had brought onto the stage and turned it over. It revealed the new company vision.

Boom! He'd nailed it. The audience loved it. The board loved it. His top team loved it. More importantly, the metaphor kept on working. Throughout the day the speakers who followed him all referred to his jigsaw puzzle. When I visited the company two months later they were still talking about the 'vision jigsaw'.

Developing and using metaphors – from the *simple metaphor* 'she was broken-hearted' to the *simile* 'Life is like a box of chocolates: you never know what you're gonna get' – is easy. My favourite is the *extended metaphor*; like the jigsaw puzzle example, it just keeps on running. It's powerful, creates a great word picture and eventually acquires a life of its own.

Edge-It

Extended metaphors keep on running and often acquire a life of their own.

A FEW WORDS OF WARNING

When a metaphor works it's because people enjoy the unique way it explains something and helps their understanding. If you pull out a tired old metaphor don't be surprised if your audience cringe. If you're not sure what a tired old metaphor looks like, here are a few you may have heard:

- It's like riding a bike . . .
- It's like a football team . . .
- It's like making a cake . . .

And if you close by saying, 'And the moral of the story is . . .', you'll lose half of your audience immediately.

When you create a metaphor, consider the core message. Try not to add on too many extraneous messages or you'll need a metaphor to explain your metaphor!

Make it visual. People like word pictures, so use a metaphor that's easily visualised; then you'll quickly get your point across. Think about JFK and Winston Churchill, two of the greatest wordsmiths of recent times. The visual language they used was brilliant:

> 'Let the word go forth from this time and place, to friend and foe alike, that the torch has been passed to a new generation of Americans.' (JFK)

> 'For a nation to tax itself into prosperity is like a man standing in a bucket and trying to lift himself up by the handle.' (Churchill)*

Be careful with analogies that involve size and scale. I recently heard someone explain the size of their product as being 'twice the height of the Eiffel Tower'. Great if you've stood at the foot of the Eiffel Tower and looked up at it, but what if you've only seen it on a postcard?

Using metaphors offers a good opportunity to add humour. With the right metaphor you are one step removed from your product, idea or concept, which makes a joke easier.

---

* Churchill also said, 'Writing a book is an adventure. To begin with, it is a toy and an amusement; then it becomes a mistress, and then it becomes a master, and then a tyrant. The last phase is that just as you are about to be reconciled to your servitude, you kill the monster, and fling him out to the public.' Hope you're enjoying the monster!

Edge-It

Your product may not have much humour, but a well-devised metaphor can help you with that.

The best way to find a metaphor that works for you is to test out your ideas with as many people as possible. Edgers are more than happy to plant the seed of a metaphor, let others nurture it, then observe the fruit of the finished idea. The more comfortable you are with telling your story, developing your word picture and linking it to your core message, the easier it becomes to create and use metaphors.

25 Selling Yourself

Everyone with the Edge can sell. Ideas, products, services and, most importantly . . . themselves.

It's a common misconception that some people are naturally good at selling. Every great salesperson I have ever met has *worked* on being able to sell, and then they execute **what they know** brilliantly.

A few years ago I employed a potential new salesperson. He had loads of enthusiasm, a jovial manner and a desire to work hard. What else do you need?

I took him to an appointment in which I was to 'pitch' to a potential new client. We knew we were meeting with the decision maker and went into the meeting brimming with confidence. It proved to be one of the best sales meetings I'd ever had. I was on fire! As we left and walked back to the car, my new apprentice was in awe. He kept pointing out how amazing I'd been, how this guy had loved our presentation and how he had wanted to buy everything. Even when we got back to our office it didn't stop there. He burst in and told everyone how brilliantly I'd performed and that we would be doing loads of business with a new client. My ego had been well and truly stroked.

Four days later I received an email from our potential new client. It read: *Dear Michael, I really enjoyed meeting with you at the start of the week. I got excited, you got excited, in fact we all got excited. But have you noticed, it's four days later, and I still haven't bought anything?*

BOOM. My heart sank. I couldn't believe it. How obvious, yet how stupid of me to assume my enthusiasm alone would be enough.

Edge-It

A great sales pitch is only great if your prospect buys something.

This lesson was delivered by our prospective client, Tim Price, a serial entrepreneur and Edger who, at that time, was building an amazing telecoms company. Even though he pointed out my mistakes, he was also happy to show me where I had gone wrong. He went on to teach me a structured sales approach; an approach that he had used for years and that, when we applied it, transformed our business.

The only downside to Tim's method was that it was very heavily geared towards 'business to business' sales; however, the framework was sound. So I further developed Tim's approach to help the clients I coached to promote themselves, their ideas and their concepts.

After some initial success I wanted to take it further, so I started to observe very 'persuasive' people to see what they did. I also studied those who can make people fall in love with their ideas. And I was especially interested in those who could encourage others to make a complete U-turn from their original position.

SELLING YOUR IDEA

Imagine you have an idea you are excited about but that you need the help of others to turn it into a reality. You know the best person (or people) to help you. What will you do to get them on board?

I'm not sure if there is an exact formula for doing this, but if there was it would look something like this:

Step One: Be So Passionate about Your Idea that You Could Burst

This is a prerequisite. You should be ridiculously excited about it. If you're not, don't bother with steps two to ten.

Step Two: Planning and Preparation

Get everything you need before you meet with the person you want to sell your idea or concept to. Just as great preparation boosts your confidence, poor preparation will take your confidence away. Here are some questions to consider as part of your preparation:

- Who are you aiming to see?
- What do you want them to do after you've seen them?
- When is the best time to see them?
- Where is the best place?
- What exactly do you need from them?
- What will they need from you?
- How can you succinctly sum up what you want?

Step Three: Meet the Right Person

YES, MEET. Don't email, write, Skype or call. Meet them. If you have to really sell an idea you must be face to face. When Tim first taught me his structured approach he called this 'Meet the MAN'. The MAN is an acronym for the person with the Money, the Authority and the Need. The most important of all these is Need. The MAN could be a woman or a man, junior or senior, old or young. Don't make the mistake of assuming you know who this person is until you've done your research.

When a person has a strong need and someone else turns up to fulfil that need, amazing things happen. Barriers come down, diaries are rescheduled and doors are opened.

It's all about how you ask for the meeting. You may be

thinking: if I was well known, rich or famous it would be easy to get a meeting with anyone. Well, how did those people start out? One of the reasons they became successful was that they would do whatever it took to get to the people who mattered. When he was just fourteen, Steve Jobs famously called the chairman of Hewlett Packard at home. He ended up giving Steve a part-time job.

Edge-It

Meet the MAN. That's the person with the MONEY, AUTHORITY and NEED.

Step Four: Fact-find and Establish Needs

The good news is you are now meeting with the person who needs to be inspired by your idea. The temptation is to launch in with both feet – sell, sell, sell! However, Edgers do something different. They make the first part of the meeting all about the person they are meeting. They ask carefully prepared questions. They show a genuine interest in what they do and how they do it. And, most importantly, they care.

Step Five: Confirmation

In Tim's structured sale model this was a test 'close'; an opportunity to see if the person you were selling to was taking the bait. If they were, it was easy to just reel them in. Selling an idea is similar but, as this is more about you, the confirmation needs to be focused on the relationship you are developing at this point.

Ask yourself: How's this going? Do I like this person? Do they like me? Are they ready for my idea? If you're getting 'yes' signs, then now's the time. Now you can share your idea.

Step Six: Share

If it's appropriate, stand up, refer back to Chapter 22: 'How to be a Super Speaker', and go for it. Have you noticed how some people are able to get you totally excited about an idea and others can turn you off before they've really got started? Provided you have followed the formula, this is the point where you share your idea or plan with a person who is wide-eyed and ready to listen. It's taken a lot to get to this point, so don't blow it now.

Edge-It

Remember, less really is more. It's a delicate balance between leaving them wanting more and giving enough information for them to make an informed decision.

That's why you need step seven.

Step Seven: Check the Temperature

During the process it's worth gauging how well your idea is going down. One of the best ways to do this is to stop for a moment, slow down and gesture that you would like some feedback. If nothing is forthcoming ask, 'How is this for you?' This is much more powerful than asking 'What do you think?' because at this point you don't want to know what they think. That comes later.

Step Eight: Final Confirmation

You are going to ask for the support of the person you are meeting with, and you are going to ask for it in a matter of minutes. This is not going to be one of those days where you get excited but end up leaving without anything concrete.

If you have followed steps one to seven correctly you should be able to incorporate everything you've learned into this final confirmation using the magic word: 'if'. It's a small word but a very powerful one. Here's how you may use 'if' as part of a final confirmation.

'As you can see, I'm passionate about this idea and I hope you have a sense of what I want to do. You need x, y, z [this being the information you picked up during step four: Fact-find]. So *if* I can provide x, y and *if* we are able to make sure z happens, would you be happy to work with me on this now?'

The reason for the word 'if' is that it allows you a little wriggle room if you need it. Should the person you are meeting with be unsure of the idea, they'll let you know. They may say, 'I need to think about it.' You'll then know that they need more information. It's worth taking a moment to ask them which part they would like to think about. You could then give them a little more information, once again using the word 'if'.

For instance a conversation may go along these lines:

'Sounds good, but I need to think about it.'

'That's fine; which part do you want to think about?'

'It's just the timing. We're at capacity at the moment.'

'Great. If I could show you why being at capacity won't be an issue and may actually enhance what we're doing, would that be beneficial?'

Edge-It

It's only two letters and a very disappointing word in Scrabble, but 'if' is one of the most important words in selling.

Step Nine: The Deal

I've been in too many meetings where I've got to step eight and never heard anything ever again – and so have you. It wasn't because there was anything wrong with you or your idea. It was probably more to do with time. The person who you were meeting with wasn't totally convinced and they believed time would help them to decide. The truth is that time can often hinder a decision. The excitement fades, the moment has gone and it all begins to feel a little flat.

To avoid this it's very important to ask for a commitment there and then, face to face. Even if you're aware you won't get their commitment, ask for it anyway. What have you got to lose?

When I was a fundraiser I learned very quickly that the best way to encourage wealthy individuals to make a big gift was to ask them for it, face to face, at a time when they were most engaged with the charity. I developed a way to do this which made it clear exactly what I was asking them for.

Edge-It

People respect clarity, and if it's true (and I believe it is) that you have one perfect moment in time – don't miss yours.

Step Ten: Review

What worked, what didn't and why? What's next? What will I do better next time?

This review process is essential. It's how the best get better. Even when everything has gone perfectly, it's essential to review what you did. Find out why it went so well. When did you know you had the other person on board?

A review is even more important when things don't go well. Go through the process. I bet if you didn't get what you wanted you missed out or messed up on one of the previous nine steps.

Didn't meet with the right person? Step three: make sure you meet the MAN. If you can't meet the MAN then your meeting has only one agenda: 'How do I persuade this person to introduce me to the MAN?'

Didn't fully connect with their needs? Step four: did you fact-find correctly? Did you ask enough of the right questions?

They just didn't get it? Step seven: Check the temperature. Was there a moment where you intuitively felt it could be going better, but your lack of confidence and fear of hearing 'no' stopped you from doing a temperature check?

Did you really understand the needs of who you were speaking to or was it just not a good fit? Perhaps as early as step two – Planning and preparation – you'd misjudged who you were seeing.

You might have the best idea in the world but if the person you are selling it to does not see how it benefits them, then you won't sell it. You may be able to manipulate the person or the situation, but resist this. They will quickly find a way to get out of their agreement and feel aggrieved. Wouldn't you rather have someone who is as excited about your idea as you are?

This step-by-step approach can be used to motivate staff for a new project, get teenagers excited about a family holiday, persuade potential investors to part with their cash, or encourage partners to spend the rest of their lives with you. Just adapt the process to the situation. For example, don't stand with a flip chart when you're trying to get the love of your life to commit to a lifetime together; you may just get the opposite result!

A final thought. Use the ten-step approach as an outline but be flexible. Sometimes you will be able to use all ten steps in a matter of hours or even minutes, other times it may take weeks. It's not perfect, but your intuition is. So there may be times when your intuition is screaming for you to do one thing but your logical brain is saying you still have two more steps to make. Go with your intuition.

26

Why Edgers Happily Pay More

Would you rather stay in a five-star or a three-star hotel?

Would you rather fly first class or economy?

Would you rather sit in the best seats at the theatre or just stand at the back?

We all want the best and we're often prepared to pay more for it. However, what you get in return for handing over the additional cash is interesting. A first-class seat isn't five times the size of an economy one? The leg room isn't five times more and the food isn't five times better. Actually, scratch that last one; five times terrible is still terrible.

What people pay for when they travel first

class is exactly what people pay more for in any area of life. Offering a service edge means providing an experience for someone that is beyond what they expected. It's the same with products or anything else. In simple terms: being that bit better, going the extra five miles and having the service Edge.

QUALITY VS LUXURY

I read a Facebook status of a friend the other day that simply said, 'I deserve luxury.' It had received lots of 'likes'. But what would you rather have: luxury or quality? You may think the two are the same but those with the Edge know there's more to it than that.

When my wife and I were first married we didn't have much money. Our TV was the portable from my bedroom, which was perched on a stool in the corner of our lounge. A couple of months into our marriage we decided we wanted to buy a video recorder, so we went to our local electrical retailer: a lovely guy called Fred Tilney. Fred really knew his stuff. Within five minutes of arriving at his shop I knew the VCR I wanted. It was the latest Hitachi with more lights and buttons than anything I'd ever seen before. My mind was made up. I wanted it and even though many of the features weren't necessary I loved the idea of owning this little bit of luxury.

After talking to Fred for a while and answering what seemed like an inordinate amount of questions we decided that we should really consider a new TV too. We later found that Fred's method of asking questions until you convinced yourself you need new stuff was one of his most graceful and clever sales approaches.

We could have chosen a standard TV but, before we made our minds up, Fred suggested we take a look at the range of high-end televisions too. As well as the usual selection of TVs and VCRs, Fred also stocked a limited range of Bang & Olufsen equipment. It was the type of kit a young fella like me drooled over. To cut a longer story short, half an hour later we'd bought a B&O TV and an amazingly thin and stylish hi-fi, as well as the Hitachi video recorder we'd originally set out to buy. Later that afternoon, after the equipment was delivered and installed, Fred said, 'I'll see you in a couple of years when you want to replace that video recorder.'

'What about the TV and the hi-fi?' I asked.

'You'll have them for ever,' he said smiling.

He was right. I can't recall when the VCR was replaced, but it was (several times) and, yes, we've had other TVs for various rooms in our home. But we still have that original Bang & Olufsen hi-fi and TV – we still use them every day. The sound and vision is amazing, the design is timeless. That's quality.

Now link that to the product or service you provide. Luxury? Quality? Both? I think you know by now how the Edger thinks. It's a classically executed combination of both. But if you had to focus on just one, I believe quality wins for the Edger. You can never provide too much quality.*

Edge-It

Often people (especially customers) need to be educated on what outstanding quality really means.

---

* My wife makes the same argument for handbags and shoes right up to the point where I say 'Well, if the design and quality is that good you'll only need three pairs and one bag then?'

Here are five things to consider when promoting quality:

1. **Longevity.** How much longer will it last? How many more uses will you get from it? What will that save you in the long term?
2. **Comfort.** The fit, leg room, seat-pitch, fabric, etc. are all nice but what's the benefit. People want comfort.
3. **Aspiration.** I once bought a car because the chairman of the biggest group of car dealerships in the UK drove the same model. The salesman said, 'My chairman can choose to drive any car in the world, but he chooses this one.'
4. **Value for money.** I don't mind paying more for better quality but it had better be worth it. Edgers hate to be ripped off, so being able to demonstrate the link between quality and value for money is essential.
5. **Saves time.** You can't buy extra time but you can buy something to save time. When quality is linked to saving time it immediately conveys a sense of convenience, which ultimately Edgers love.

Most people are happy to pay more if they feel happy with what they get in return. The Edger knows this and uses it to their advantage when they're selling and promoting their goods, services and that all-important aspirational experience.

27

Making Others Feel Fab

I

If there's one thing that Edgers don't experience it's being on edge, or making others feel on edge.

Being in the company of someone with the Edge is effortless. You may have thought it would be difficult, but it's not. Every truly successful person I've met has the ability to instantly make you feel at ease.

LESSONS FROM FOOTBALL

I was a fundraiser for many years working for two charities. The first was a children's health charity that relied on mass events involving thousands of volunteers. The average donation from individuals was less than £10 per head but we raised a staggering £12 million. When you're a fundraiser, that's a huge task. It was during this time that I was lucky enough to meet Kevin Keegan.

Park what you think about football for a moment and consider Kevin Keegan as a person. He is well known for wearing his heart on his sleeve (YouTube him and watch 'I'd love it if we beat them') and being passionate about people and communities. And the good news for us was that when he became manager of Newcastle United he also became a supporter of our charity.

I met him on several occasions and always marvelled at the way he made everyone feel totally at ease. He would arrive at an event full of nervous people and by the time he left everyone would remark what a great guy he was.

If I'd known I'd be writing this book twenty years later I would have spent a little longer studying what made Mr Keegan so special, but I did ask him once why he thought he was so popular. After a slight hesitation, in a quiet voice he said, 'I work at it.'

Edge-It

People who have the ability to make others feel totally at ease may appear to do it naturally. Most often, they've worked hard at it.

Each year our charity held an event called Families of Courage, which celebrated and recognised people who had faced hardship and trauma. The year he took over as manager, we invited sixteen families from across the north of England, some of whom had children with extremely challenging health issues. We asked Kevin if he would be our guest of honour for the event. Of course he said yes.

A function room was booked, and on the big day we had almost a hundred guests . . . but no Kevin Keegan. We weren't worried as he'd sent a message from the training ground explaining that there had been some issues that morning but he was definitely coming. When he arrived, he was forty minutes late. He paced into the room, took the microphone and said, 'I'm so sorry I'm late. We've been training this morning and a couple of things happened that held me up. I wanted to see if I could make it up to you so I've invited a few friends to join me here today. Here's Lee Clark, Robbie Elliott, Philippe Albert, Andy Cole . . .'

He went on to introduce the entire Newcastle United squad, having insisted that they should give up an hour or two of their time to come to the event. I remember watching him that afternoon as he met all the kids and their parents. He made sure our volunteers felt special; he also gave the same time and attention to the press, the AV guys and the hotel staff. He was the last to leave, having made sure he had connected with everyone.

It's easy to say that Edgers like Kevin Keegan have a natural charisma, but let me assure you they work on it too.

So if Kevin Keegan does work harder at it, what is he working on?

Here are five simple ways to make people feel fabulous:

1. Be interested. And I mean really interested. People with the Edge are genuinely interested in others.

2. Have some questions ready. I'm surprised by people who don't know what to ask in conversation. 'I don't know what to ask' should never be a reason for not asking.

   Let's starts with the Royal family's favourite: 'What do you do?' This is often the only question you need. I ask it like this: 'So what do you do in real life?' It raises a smile and gives people an opportunity to talk about anything.

   'What are you focusing on right now?' is an-other. I prefer this to 'What are you working on?'

3. Keep the right amount of eye contact. I once went on a course where the advice was to 'maintain eye contact'. This kind of freaks people out after a while, so work on focusing on the other person just enough. Don't freak them out.

4. Hold on just a little bit longer. If you shake hands. hold on just a little longer. If you're meeting someone you know well and are giving them a hug, again hold on just a little longer. Some people feel slightly uncomfortable with touch. Most Edgers don't.

5. Remember this. *No one cares how much you know until they know how much you care.* This is a mantra I share all the time with everyone. People really don't care that you may have a load of technical information, nor about what you've achieved or even what you do, unless they know that you care about them first.

Edge-It

Edgers get others involved, especially at events. They are always the ones introducing people to each other, and in doing so they make both parties feel special.

On the flipside, I bet you've met someone who made you feel small and insignificant. I wanted to share a story in this chapter about a person from the world of football who made me feel totally insignificant. I wrote it and gave it to my wife Christine for her thoughts. She asked what benefit it would serve by naming him and telling the awful story. I made my point that he was someone who thought he had the Edge but really hasn't. She then brilliantly commented, 'This is a chapter about how to make people feel fab. Will it make anyone feel better reading a story about how awful someone was? And what if he reads the book?'

She does have a habit of being right, my wife.

The next time you're out and about meeting people, think about the positive or negative impact you may be having on them. Every word, question, gesture and expression makes a difference.

Edge-It

Ask yourself what type of individual you want to be known as, then make your actions and behaviours fit that person.

28

Fear of Firing

When I was research-ing this book I spent time interviewing an old friend, Jack Krellé; his wisdom is dotted throughout these pages. Of course he denies having the Edge, but he finds it easy to identify with what the Edgers have in common.

A few weeks before my deadline, he sent me an email suggesting the subject for my next book, developing on the theme of *The Edge*. He called it *Fear of Firing*.

The premise was simple: most people have a fear of firing. They would rather put up with mediocrity than challenge someone and, if necessary, fire them. I'm a massive action person, and the thought of waiting for my next book was just too much, so here's my (and a bit of Jack's) thinking now.

Mediocrity has become the mainstream and the main culprits are the leaders who have allowed this to happen. Mediocre managers, slack suppliers and silent customers have conspired to make less than the best acceptable.

Let's take each one, break it down, see why most people have a fear of firing, and look at what the Edgers do about it.

MANAGERS

The huge challenge with most managers is their belief that they have to act in a certain way to be popular. The truth is one of the most brilliant paradoxes in management: by trying to be popular you actually become less popular. Ricky Gervais brilliantly parodied this in *The Office* with David Brent (and in the US series of the same name, with Michael Scott played by Steve Carell). In fact Ricky Gervais did it so well that many people thought *The Office* was real, referencing their own cringeworthy experiences with managers to the David Brent character.

No one would admit to being like Brent, but the truth is that many managers have some of the traits of the Slough stationery supplier's worst asset. The problem with David Brent was that he really did want to do a good job. He wanted people to enjoy coming to work and feel like one big happy family. It's just that his team didn't. They had families outside of the office, didn't want to wear their hearts on their sleeves and certainly didn't want their boss to be their best mate.

Edge-It

There's a thin (very thin) line between 'caring boss' and 'hapless idiot', and that line is getting thinner.

Bosses are terrified of upsetting their team or, in some cases, being hauled before a disciplinary panel (or even court) because they said or did the wrong thing. Therefore it's got to be easier to be mates with everyone. Your mates wouldn't sue you, would they?

So there's the dilemma. The same person you were down the pub with yesterday is the one who's under-performing today. How can you possibly criticise the person who just twenty-four hours earlier was admiring pictures of your kids and sharing a bag of ready salted? The answer is simple, but not easy. Edgers mark out the parameters in their minds first. Then they communicate them to those who they manage, work with and work for. Then – and this is the key part – they act on it and gracefully know where to draw the line.

When my dad was running his roofing business it was traditional for the lads to finish early and join him for a drink on the last Friday before Christmas. It was his business and his decision to pay his employees to spend the afternoon in the pub. I worked for him for seven years, and it was only in the last couple that I worked out what his strategy was. He would come to the pub, insist on buying the first round, order a shandy for himself, then make sure he had a couple of minutes chat with each of the lads. Then he would quietly go home. Compare that to what David Brent would do.

I'm not saying you shouldn't go to the pub with your team. I am suggesting you should know where your line is and what it would take for you to cross it. My father had very clear parameters that he stood by. He was a tough boss and there were times when I witnessed him being *very* explicit in his expectations of his employees. But he was a boss who had respect. Last year my father died and at his funeral, which was packed with people who had worked for him, I was touched by the number of former employees (tough slaters and builders) who commented on how they had 'more respect for him than anyone I have ever worked for', 'always known exactly where I stood with your dad' and, most touchingly, 'loved Bill'.

My dad did have to fire a few people in his time and there wasn't one who was surprised or didn't think they deserved it. How would you fare with having to fire someone? Even the word 'fired' feels nasty, even more so since it became the catch-phrase of *The Apprentice*. However, it's a lot easier to get rid of poor performers in *The Apprentice* than it is in real life. With a point of the finger, Lord Sugar declares, 'You're fired', and they're gone. They shuffle out of the boardroom and into the waiting cab.

Can you imagine Lord Sugar or Donald Trump finishing the show with, 'Chris, you're . . . going to have a performance review, which will be carried out by HR and closely monitored by the legal department. We'll have weekly meetings where I'll pretend to be interested in your workflow while the truth is I'll actually be smarting about the fact that it will take another six of these blessed meetings and a further three months before I can get rid of you without you suing the business. That's the same business which has paid your inflated salary for the last few years of your outstanding under-performance. And that's mainly because your manager didn't tackle the problem with you. Probably as they were too busy down the pub looking at your kids' photos and sharing packets of ready salted crisps.'

When I coach senior people, especially ones in long-established organisations, we often get round to the question of what to do about people who are under-performing. I offer them a few simple questions that invariably help them to get to where they need to be.

- **Is their position crucial?** If it isn't it can make getting rid of them much easier.
- **How important are they to your mission-critical activity?** The key here is *mission critical* as opposed to day to day. You can get by without day to day for a while; mission critical takes a little more care.
- **Is this a blip or permanent behaviour?** Blips can be fixed, but only if you are prepared to roll up your sleeves and get involved. Behaviours, on the other hand, are more challenging and much more difficult

to change. This doesn't mean they can't be changed; it's just that the level of energy needed to change them is huge. And that assumes they are open to a behavioural shift.

- **What have you done to rectify it?** I'm constantly amazed by the number of people who have a problem member of their team and whose strategy in dealing with this has been to *hope* they'll change. This is one of those occasions where hope is not a strategy. If, on the other hand, you've tried courses, coaching, me time, group time, reiki, residentials, Myers Briggs, Tony Robbins, KPIs, KPMG, books, videos, audios, part time, flexi-time, full time, no time, psychiatry, psychology, sociology, stretch targets, SMART goals, daily boosts, *laissez-faire*, being democratic, autocratic, systematic and hydromatic (see *Grease*), dress-down Friday, dress-up Monday, naked Wednesday, seven effective habits, six thinking hats, five-star service, Mind Maps, boot camps, Outward Bound, orienteering and intervention, and you're still not getting anywhere, then perhaps it is time to let them go.
- **What are you prepared to spend to fix this?** A senior HR director assured me she could remove any member of staff without any repercussions so

long as the money was right. It's worth considering how much it's costing you emotionally and financially to keep problems in your team and setting a 'budge budget' to remove the ones who really shouldn't be there.

You've guessed it, Edgers know this. Which is why they rarely find themselves in this situation. The exception being when they have inherited an existing team. But even if they do end up managing a team with some dead wood in it, you can be sure they'll act swiftly to deal with the situation.

One of my massive-action coaching clients removed 30 per cent of poor performers during his first six months in post. He's since replaced them with high performers. When I asked him about the process, he commented that it was the 70 per cent who remained who were the most interesting. 'They've raised their game; they had to!'

Of course many managers don't want to take these steps. Their need for social capital far outweighs their desire for any rational commitment to the progress of the organisation. Could *you* sack someone who you have as a Facebook friend?

And what if you're not performing as well as you could? It's hard enough to challenge someone on their performance when you're at the top of your own game, but what happens when your personal performance could be better. It's tough, and it's a heck of a lot harder than having a team of mates who stick up for you and cover your foibles.

Edge-It

Managers with the Edge relentlessly tackle under-performance and do whatever it takes to ensure they have the strongest, leanest, most effective team.

SUPPLIERS AND PARTNERS

It goes beyond staff. Poor suppliers and partners are driving people nuts. Yes, we complain about our energy provider, bank, garage, schools, elected representatives, etc., but rarely will we actually do anything about it.

I know someone who cleans before and after their cleaner! Yes, read that again – before and after. I'm sure most people who are fortunate enough to have a cleaner have prepared and tidied before their cleaner comes (usually to avoid embarrassment) but not cleaned afterwards! When I challenged her on why she didn't just ask the cleaner to do it the way she wanted, she told me, 'I did try to once, but she looked really upset so, to keep the peace, I just keep my mouth shut. Now I've got to the point where it's been going on for so long there's nothing I can do about it.'

You may have read that quote and thought, 'That's crazy;

just tell her. You're paying for that service', but I dare bet there's something similar happening in your life too.

Who provides a service or product you could be happier with? Write a list of your suppliers and partners and then tick all the ones you're thrilled with, leave those which are just OK, and put a cross next to those you really could be happier with. Then take action.

Challenge all the ones with a cross. Either give them an ultimatum (one which you will follow through on) or switch. You know you'll feel better when it's done, so start with a couple of simple ones to get started.

Edge-It

One final thought on suppliers and partners. You get what you pay for. Edgers may be careful, but they're not tight.

SILENT CUSTOMERS

These are the ones who can fire you and you won't even know. 'Beware the Silent Customer' is a chapter from my book, *5 Star Service*. It was designed to point out the pitfalls of thinking that customers are happy if they're not complaining. The truth is, we've all had one of those experiences where we weren't a happy customer. We didn't complain at the time; we just made a mental note that the experience was disappointing and hoped it wouldn't happen again.

The Edge

So what do the Edgers do? It's a 50/50 split between those who complain and those who don't. However, those who don't complain will take action to ensure they never find themselves in that situation again. They'll change, switch or find someone new, rather than give the providers of poor service another chance. They're like silent assassins: you won't even know they've fired you until it's too late.

The Edgers who do complain are often very vocal and direct, but they also tend to give second chances. Breaking this down, they believe that (as a customer) if they do complain AND tell the airline/restaurant/hotel manager exactly what they could do better, the service should improve. So the next time they take the flight, eat the meal, stay in the hotel, they'll expect to see an improvement.

This behaviour (thinking) is unusual for the Edger. They want to control their level of service and, by pointing out what's wrong and what could be better, they hope to ultimately improve it. However, at the same time, they realise that service levels can often be difficult to improve due to changes of staff, not meeting with the key influencers, etc.

Mediocrity is despised by Edgers so much that one of their key priorities is to challenge it and encourage others to raise their game, just as they themselves do. It's a never-ending cycle of moving to the next level, exhibiting continuous improvement and expecting those around them to do the same.

Edge-It

Whether you're the CEO of a billion-dollar business or a consumer with a niggle, it's your right to demand improvement. However, only expect real results if you're willing to participate fully.

Don't expect others to raise their game if you're happy to sit back and watch while the world changes around you. In reading this book I'm happy to assume which camp you're in.

29

Over
the
Edge

Where there's light there's shade. Where there's Yin there's Yang. And where there's a wonderful side to having the Edge there's a dark side too. It would be remiss of me not to take some time to share with you some of the conflicts that Edgers face. Many of these foibles come with the package; some are specific to

certain Edgers and some are tiny eccentricities that eventually affect them all. It's so often the case that the Edger doesn't even recognise they have a 'dark side'. And if they are aware, they'll largely choose to ignore it, claiming it's no big deal and remaining convinced that all the brilliant stuff they do far outweighs the negatives.

The purpose of this book is to help you to find your Edge, not for you to emulate someone else's. However, in finding your Edge there are a few basic pointers to keep a check on and ensure they don't happen to you. Here's a list of the top 'Anti Edge' traits to avoid.

TOO FOCUSED

Is it possible to be too focused? Yes! Some Edgers are so focused they can't see what's happening right in front of their faces. They neglect the subtle clues that suggest they should change. The problem with being too focused on one thing is that everything else becomes blurred.

A LACK OF TOLERANCE

Edgers can quickly become intolerant of others who don't think in the same way, act as quickly or have the same intellect as they do. They'll display insensitivities, often appear cold and standoffish and become increasingly frustrated, failing to consider multiple intelligences. That is, until they need someone with complementary skills to their own.

I remember once meeting a mole catcher; he came to an open meeting to learn how to promote a new telephone service. The mole-catching business wasn't what it had been and he needed a little extra money. I liked him but a couple at the event weren't quite so keen. They thought it 'really brought the business down' having him around. Move on a couple of months when I received a phone call from one of them asking if I had the phone number of the mole catcher. They'd woken that morning to find their beautiful half-acre of lawn full of molehills. He went to their house the same day, solved their problem and quickly became their hero and new best friend.

Edge-It

Be careful: the person you show a lack of tolerance to today could be your champion tomorrow.

THE NEED TO BE RIGHT

Once anyone becomes a leading expert in anything, their opinion is taken as indisputable fact. The challenge is that being right about your chosen subject is never enough for you; you'll always want more. One of the negatives of some Edgers is that they consider being wrong a sign of weakness – and they never want to show any signs of weakness.

The prospect of saying, 'I don't know' or, worse still, 'I was wrong' is just too much. Instead, they skirt around the issue, make excuses and say ridiculous things like, 'That's what I meant' or 'That's what I was going to say.'

Edge-It

If you're wrong, suck it up. Admit to it. Find out what's right and then learn from it.

IN DENIAL

I don't want to get into a deep psychological discussion about why some Edgers end up in denial, so I'll just suggest that some do. And they find it very difficult to accept that it's a behavioural problem. But what about the effect being in denial has on other people? Here are some classic in-denial behaviours from Edgers:

- Refusing to admit to their age: the belief that they have to look younger or say they're younger than they actually are.
- Refusing to accept the failings of other family members, especially children: it's never their kids who caused the problem, did the bullying, missed the lesson, failed the exam, etc; it must be down to the school or the teacher.

- Refusing to accept that their ideas aren't as unique as they'd like to think they are: 'That competitor will never be as good as us' – when in fact they're already on their way to being better.
- Refusing to look honestly at their weight and health: 'I think I'm doing well considering my age and how busy I am.'
- Refusing to face up to why people don't like them: 'It's because I've been so successful. People are jealous.'

It's difficult when you have the Edge to accept that some other parts of your life may not be quite as perfect as you'd like to think they are.

DISSATISFIED

Even when they have achieved great things, Edgers can still be dissatisfied. Five great cars aren't enough. 'That model is twelve months old and now they've launched a new one.' 'The tickets for the event were good . . . but that next row forward seemed to have an even better view.'

Because 'it's never quite right' they focus on the bits that are wrong and in doing so create even more discontent. This is a vicious circle that can lead to someone who, on the face of it, has everything being incredibly unhappy. And consider the effect that has on their nearest and dearest.

A POOR LIFE BALANCE

Don't ever lose sight of why you strive for success and recognition. Tell me you'll never put yourself in the situation where you say, 'Yes, I've found my Edge – I'm No. 1. However, to get there I've had two heart attacks, my partner left me, the kids won't talk to me, I've lost my life savings and most (well all) of my mates. I'm known as a ruthless bastard, who'll do whatever it takes, even if it means working eighteen hours a day, seven days a week, and using the odd dodgy substance to keep me awake. I'm notorious for abusing the people around me, being wasteful and boring, and I lack any kind of spirituality. But that's OK because I'm No. 1.'

Edge-It

Keep checking in with your life balance at least once a month (use The Wheel of Life at www.michaelheppell.com) and if you spot a blip, do something about it – quickly.

AN UNCONTROLLABLE EGO

This is a tricky one because to get the Edge you need a bit of ego. The challenge is when it becomes uncontrollable and feeding the ego becomes all-consuming. Then, if it doesn't get fed by one method, it searches for other sources to fulfil its craving.

I know someone who had put on a considerable amount of weight and wanted to lose it. As she lost weight her ego was boosted by the many positive comments that people made. Every week she would report on her progress and, in so doing, increase the number of positive comments she received. This was perfect. Her ego was boosted, she became slimmer, felt amazing and was motivated to lose more weight. So she continued to lose weight week after week for over a year.

The challenge occurred when she hit her target weight. The people closest to her soon got used to her new figure and the positive comments were greatly reduced. Her ego wasn't being fed. The good news was that she didn't go back to eating for comfort, but the bad news was that her ego was hungry and she didn't know when enough was enough. When meeting a new person she would steer the conversation towards food or weight loss and at the first opportunity pull out a photograph she kept in her handbag of how she had looked a few years earlier. Her ego was boosted (fed) momentarily but for those around her she sounded like a broken record. She needed help to change her focus.

One of the greatest challenges Edgers face is the amount of effort they need to put in to create and maintain the publicity that feeds their ego. To do this they project an image, sometimes far removed from their authentic self. It feels good, feeds their ego, and so they crave for more. Sooner or later they hit the danger zone and start to believe their own publicity. Then, not only do those around them grow tired of them but they themselves struggle to find their true identity.

Edge-It

As hip-hop group Public Enemy said, 'Don't believe the hype!'

FORGETTING WHERE YOU'RE FROM

What you did to get from B to C wasn't the same stuff you did to get from A to B and is completely different from what you'll do to get from C to D. And the people you come into contact with will be different too. So make sure you don't forget those who were with you when you started. Remember the ones who helped you during the early days.

This is a common fault of Edgers. They find it difficult to maintain relationships with people from the earlier parts of their lives, especially professionally, so they cut them off altogether. They don't realise that (in most cases) the people who were around for them during their early days don't expect them to be the same person now as they were then. They're happy about their success and expected them to change.

CRAVING PUBLICITY

Edgers can get caught in the trap of courting publicity but then hating it when they get it. This is frequently demonstrated in the world of entertainment. The aspiring actor or singer is desperate to promote themselves, so they set up stunts and 'their people' arrange for the press to be there. A media furore ensues and their career rides on the back of it. When they've made it, the press wants more from them but they no longer want or need the publicity as badly. And especially not the negative stuff.

Most Edgers know that if you want and set out to gain publicity you will get it. Some of it good and some of it bad, and it's unlikely they'll be in equal measures. Craving publicity and wanting to control it (another trait of the Edger) is unrealistic and will never work.

BEING A LOUSY LEADER

Their drive got them started, their vision built their business, but now a different set of skills are needed to lead. Many Edgers are described as born leaders but, for some, leading is a chore that they are just not cut out for.

When someone thinks they know how to lead but doesn't, it's a recipe for disaster. They try to lead, but instead of creating followers they create dissenters. And on top of this, there's a healthy dose of self-denial. When staff leave the business, the Edger never considers it's their own leadership ability that needs to be questioned; it's the capacity of the staff member, who just couldn't stick the pace.

BEING GREEDY

They want it all. They worked hard. They took the knocks along the way, so they deserve it, right? You can't blame someone for wanting more but there has to be time to ask the question, 'How much is enough?'

Edge-It

Edgers can quickly move from ambitious and hard-working to ruthless and greedy in a few badly thought-out moves.

INSECURITY

Superficially Edgers are the most confident people on the planet. In reality, lack of confidence is the Achilles heel of many of them. They are riddled with self-doubt, extremely suspicious of other people's motives, and fear losing what they have to the extent that they rarely entirely enjoy their success.

A few years ago I worked with a Premiership footballer who seemingly had it all. A successful career, recognition, real talent, loyal fans and £40,000 a week. In truth, he was in constant fear of being dropped from the team and hated being recognised – so much so that he would rarely leave his house and would wear a disguise should he do so. He'd beat himself up over the tiniest mistake, was worried that his fans would turn on him, and had sleepless nights thinking that his close family members were after his money.

If you suffer from insecurity now, getting the Edge won't fix it; your insecurity will be exacerbated. Really successful Edgers spend as much time working on their self-confidence as they do working on their practical skills.

BEING BAD-TEMPERED

With the Edge comes pressure. Some Edgers are able to handle the pressure brilliantly. They stay calm, relaxed and feel happy. Others don't. They feel the stress physically and become increasingly bad-tempered. They justify this by pointing out just how much they have to deal with, the challenges they face in their lives and the incompetence of others. Rather than make time for quiet contemplation or self-reflection, they become defensive. And the challenge with this strategy is that it works! When someone is bad-tempered the people around them tend to tread more carefully, be more understanding and give them more space. What the Edger needs is someone they trust to be honest with them.

THINKING YOU'RE IRREPLACEABLE

As soon as an Edger thinks they are inimitable they're in trouble. It's dangerous to assume that there isn't someone just as good or better than you (with a better attitude), who's almost ready to take your crown. Sports, business, entertainment and politics are littered with examples of people who thought they were irreplaceable. Who could forget the face of Margaret Thatcher when she was forced to resign as prime minister in 1990?

Edge-It

Thinking you are irreplaceable feeds arrogance. Arrogance breeds contempt. Contempt gets you sacked. And if you're reading this and thinking you can't be sacked . . .

PUBLICLY CRITICISING THE PEOPLE WHO SUPPORT YOU

On 18 June 2010 England played Algeria in the World Cup finals. It should have been a simple (never easy) win for England. For many fans this trip was to be the highlight of their years of unstinting support. They had saved to travel to South Africa to follow their team to victory. Instead they were left devastated by a lacklustre performance and a 0–0 draw. So the highly emotional England supporters booed their team off the pitch at the final whistle. Leaving the field, Wayne Rooney turned to the live camera and, rather than apologising for his part in the debacle, filled the air with venom by snarling at and criticising the fans, saying, 'It's nice to see your own fans booing you . . . that's what loyal support is. For f**k's sake.'

If there was ever a way to lose your Edge, he demonstrated it brilliantly.

Gerald Ratner, the then chief executive of the jewellers Ratner's, did it famously in business when, in front of the Institute of Directors, he held up one of his products and said,

'We also do cut-glass sherry decanters complete with six glasses on a silver-plated tray that your butler can serve you drinks on, all for £4.95. People say, "How can you sell this for such a low price?" I say, "Because it's total crap."'

To make matters worse he said that some of the ear-rings they sold were 'cheaper than a Marks & Spencer's prawn sandwich but probably wouldn't last as long'. After the speech, which had been recorded and was broadcast to millions, the value of the Ratner's group plummeted by around £500 million.

And one more snippet to drive home the point. You would hope that David Shepherd, as the brand director for Top Man clothing, would want to make his customers feel proud of their buying decisions. When he was asked to identify the target market for Top Man suits he said, 'Hooligans or whatever. Very few of our customers have to wear suits for work. They'll be for his first interview or first court case.'

Amazingly, out of the three, only Ratner lost his job.

Edgers are human. They make mistakes, upset people, get things wrong, focus on the wrong stuff, feel sad, get mad and let their egos take over. This chapter hasn't been written to put you off finding your Edge; it's more a map of the minefield you might face, to help you chart your way safely through it.

30
Massive
Action

TripAdvisor is a rapidly growing company with a powerful philosophy that originates from their founder and prolific Edger, Stephen Kaufer.

It's simple: Speed Wins.

Kaufer argues that one of the keys to his company's success is the ability to make fast decisions and implement them. And that's not just his or the senior team's stance: the philosophy runs throughout the whole company.

The Edge

Projects last for just two or three days, meetings take place quickly and stuff gets done. Their 'speed wins' philosophy reads like this:

'Speed wins — no if, and or buts'

Kaufer has a 'speed wins' sign on his door. It's used as part of the company's recruitment process. And it's part of every product and service they provide. So whether you're writing code in the back office or launching the latest marketing campaign, 'speed wins' will be a fundamental part of the way you work.

Exciting isn't it?

I've been using the phrase 'massive action equals massive results' for years. It's the type of phrase that people pick up on and like to repeat. It's easy to say but is it as easy to do?

Edge-It

All Edgers take massive action – it's part of their DNA.

The more you meet people with the Edge, the more you realise that this trait is key to their success. Here's a selection of the things they take massive action on.

PHYSICAL

From the speed they walk to the way they talk it's all just that little bit faster. Edgers think everyone else is just going slower when in reality they're going faster. Walking from their car to the office is quicker. They'll appear almost always in a 'hurry'.

CALLS

Most people associate telephone calls with taking a long time and so, instead, they choose to email. This takes hours and slows decision making down. For the Edger the telephone is there to make calls and get things done. They don't spend unnecessary time on the phone; their calls are focused and to the point. They don't feel the need to chat for long periods of time, which is where most people lose their pace. They make their call; it's succinct and well mannered; then they find a polite way to say goodbye.

MEETINGS

Edgers are happy to have meetings so long as their time is being used wisely. Their frustration comes when a meeting that could take five minutes is stretched out to an hour – because that's what's in the diary. That's why you'll find most Edgers like to lead meetings. They'll lead them with purpose and pace, still allowing everyone to have their say but always maintaining a firm control of the clock and the agenda.

TIMESCALES

As you would expect, those with the Edge have completely different timescales to other people. It's not unusual for them to want to halve the time that any task takes. They become terribly frustrated when projects over-run.

Edge-It

Edgers almost always manage to shave time off projects and, in doing so, set new expectations that impact all of us.

Most recently, this has been seen with building projects. Chinese company Broad Sustainable Buildings has taken this to a whole new level, building a thirty-storey (yes thirty-storey) hotel in just three hundred and sixty hours (fifteen days). Not only was it an incredibly fast construction, but the hotel is also breaking records for being more environmentally friendly, safer and economic than others built at the same time. Broad Sustainable Buildings has another ambitious goal: they are aiming to build the second-tallest building in the world – in just six months.

PERMANENT PERPETUAL PUSHING

Those three P's are shared in common by everyone who has the Edge. They just keep pushing, they're not going to let it go, they're tireless. They're like a dog with a bone. They just keep at it.

If necessary, they will repeat the same things over and over again until others get it. Whether it's a question, a task, a way of working or anything that will move things forward faster, they have a way of staying with it long after others would quit.

Not pushing for perfection, but pushing to make things better. Continuous improvement.

Their pushing can either be motivating or daunting, depending on the type of person who's on the other end of the push. Skilled Edgers recognise this and adapt appropriately. They often surround themselves with colleagues who work in a similar manner. As a team they live, eat and breathe continuous improvement and, as a result, everyone gets better.

The impression these pacemakers give is that they will do almost anything to get things done. It gives clients confidence and colleagues something to aspire to. However, it can be tiring for those who are closest to them away from a work environment. If two people in a relationship move through life with that level of pace, they must make sure they are in step with each other. If one, or both, begins to move at a different speed, their relationship will rapidly collapse.

Edge-It

The downside to this way of working is that it's so focused it's easy to miss everything else that's going on: real life!

So, a word of warning: knowing when to slow down is just as important as knowing when to speed things up. Massive correct action is brilliant, and when you focus on the right things you will get massive results. But there's a whole world out there and sometimes just slowing down, appreciating the moment and enjoying life is all the massive action you need.

31

After the Edge

S

o that's it. You've read the book, explored every chapter and challenged your thinking. What's next?

Edgers always take time to review, so let's spend a final couple of minutes to do that. And I'd like you to have two questions in mind as you do this:

- What have I learned?
- What will I do?

But first, a declaration. I'm happy to admit that the Edge is full of contradictions. In one chapter you'll read of the strengths and qualities of those described as Edgers and in the next some of their well-known traits are portrayed as things to avoid.

When writing this book I was initially frustrated by these contradictions, wondering if I should find other examples. However, the more I immersed myself in the world of the Edgers the more I became fascinated by them and particularly their contradictions. This is what makes them human. And when you realise that people with the Edge are just people – yes, people like you and me, who make mistakes, get annoyed, have the odd bad day and wish for what they can't have – then the idea of finding your own Edge comes that little bit closer.

You'll have guessed by now that true Edgers are different. They think and act differently. Not in a barmy way; rather, they have an uncanny ability to walk the line between genius and eccentric which makes them not just interesting, but fascinating.

So my first question for you after reading *The Edge* is this. Are you fascinating? Are you the type of person who people are intrigued by? Do you leave a lasting impression? If you've just given yourself a big tick then congratulations, you're part of a very small group of people who believe they are fascinating.

So maybe having the Edge is a gift. Are you born with it? Well, the nature versus nurture argument could rip through these pages – but I didn't think that would help you to find your Edge. What I do know is that everyone with the Edge has taken what they have – whether they were born with it, were given it or learned it – and built on it. This desire to be better through the acquisition of additional skills and knowledge is really one of the keys that sets the Edger apart.

So my next question is: what are you doing to acquire the skills and knowledge you need to find your Edge? Have you scheduled what you need to learn next? Are you as fascinated now as you've ever been? Do you have a thirst for knowledge? If not, perhaps it's because you haven't found the right knowledge to be thirsty for . . . yet.

Edgers seem to stick around for a little longer than others, too. Yes, the vast majority of Edgers take care of themselves. It's not about religiously hitting the gym seven days a week and leading a life of abstinence; it's simply understanding the principles of Eat Well, Think Well and Move Well.

It's no coincidence that studies into how to have a long, healthy and happy life keep coming up with the same formula. You can find it in these pages, but to save you some time, here's a summary:

Move – Walk and move quickly and with purpose. Be active for most of the day and do things faster. From making a cake to painting the fence, throw yourself into activities.

Down-time – Balance your activity (mental and physical) and understand the value of quality down-time. Schedule this into your life as a ritual and enjoy regular breaks.

Eat wisely – It's often as much about the way you eat as what you eat: knowing when enough is enough, and really savouring food rather than just shovelling it in. Take time to prepare meals, eat as a family and eat at a table without the distraction of a TV.

Stay connected – Healthy Edgers connect with others; they're social, interested and happy to share. They belong to communities and play their part. They will often have the same group of lifelong friends.

Sense of purpose – The two most dangerous years of your life (and I'm talking about death here) are the year that you're born and the year you retire. Edgers rarely retire. They find so much purpose in what they do that when one career ends they start looking for the next challenge to keep them physically active and mentally fit.

Focus on those five areas and you'll be a happy Edger and add years to your life.

As well as sharing inspirational stories of Edgers with you, I've also attempted to add a few 'How to's' along the way. Some involve exercises that I've challenged you to do as soon as you've read them. If you're like 95 per cent of people you probably won't have done them – yet. You'll tell yourself that you'll come back to them or do them later when you have a pen. Here's a tip. Decide now when you're going to do the exercises, schedule that time and make a commitment to see it through. Take away the 'should' and make it a 'must'.

And while we're on the subject of musts, one of the underlying traits of Edgers is that when they need to do something they always make it a must. Non-Edgers (and I can't believe I've waited until the last chapter to use that term) become incredibly proficient in explaining why something didn't happen or why they were unable to do this or that. To get your Edge, make sure you use 'musts' and make it happen. Using 'must' is key to your future success.

It's weird when you get to this stage of writing a book and you're challenged with how to finish it. Do you go for a rambling summary of every chapter, dispersed with personal challenges, or do you try to be clever and link it all together into one killer *must do* which would leave you, the reader, reaching for an action planner? Or, if I get it wrong, leave you reaching for a bucket. Too risky.

So here's my plan. I'm going to finish just as I started. The Edge was designed to be a study into how the best get better. I've attempted to peel back some of the layers and reveal what they, the very best, think and do. I believe that after a year of research and six months of writing I've scratched the surface, added a couple of dents and once or twice uncovered the core. And it's that fundamental principle I'd like to end on.

So, as you begin your journey to do what it takes – taking massive action and challenging yourself and others to find your Edge – keep that core in mind, because my conclusion is simply this: those who have the Edge, and I mean really have the Edge, are nice people. Kind people with good hearts and pure souls.

And that's why I sincerely hope you find your Edge.

Thank You.

There are so many people to thank in a project such as this, including a whole bunch who happily gave their time but didn't want to be named. So, first of all, to those people a huge thank you for your time and your modesty.

The Edge

Now the really tough part. Do you read the credits at the end of a movie and think, what did all of those people do? And do you know that not all of the people involved in making a movie are listed in the final credits? So you've worked out that I'm basically preparing anyone who thinks they should be in this list, and who I've inadvertently missed out, for their inevitable disappointment.

So, in no particular order (other than the first one) here we go:

Christine Heppell – Amazing Co-writer and Wonderful Wife

Vanessa Thompson – Queen of Organisation

Ruth Thomson – Duchess of Sales

Sheila Storey – Queen Mother of Money

Alastair Walker – King of Communication

Sarah Heppell – Princess of Philosophies

Laura Scott – Empress of Everything

Rowena Webb – Perfect Publisher

Maddy Price – Editor With The Edge

Jim Caunter – Persuasive Proof Reader

Danny Meyer – America's Greatest Restaurateur

Jonathan Raggett – World's Greatest Hotelier

Steve Walker – Turnaround Tsar

Irene Dorner – Perfect People Person

Jack Krellé – Insight Interrogator

Davina McCall – Emotion Educator

Patrick Kielty – Super-smart Satirist

Beatrice Tollman – Service Inspirer

Suze Orman – The Money Lady

John Elliott – Principled Philanthropist

Peter Field – Enseignant de la vie

General Sir Mike Jackson – Army Authority
Tim Brownson – Lively Life Coach
Simon Woodroffe – YO! YO! YO!
Pratap Shirke – Modest Mogul
William Baker – Never Trust A Stylist
Alex Holiday – Lean Manufacturer
Scott Sherwood – Intellect Investigator
Fred Tilney – Sensory Stimulator
Caspar Berry – Risk Reverser
Michael Foster – Secret Agent
Annabel Murello – Deal Maker
Karen Geary – Consummate Communicator
Bea Long – Permission Persuader
Tim Price – Structured Seller
Rachael Stock – Thought Police
Richard Nugent – Lads Lunch Leader
Philip Ball – Sound Originator

Michael Heppell
Keynote Speaker

Book Michael to present *The Edge* as a motivational keynote for your organisation.

Contact Michael Heppell Ltd

Email: info@michaelheppell.com
Website: michaelheppell.com

Telephone: UK 08456 733 336
Overseas +44 1434 688 555

Twitter: @michaelheppell
Facebook: facebook.com/michaelheppellofficial

Free Bonus Chapter

Visit www.michaelheppell.com/The-Edge and you can download a free bonus chapter featuring more Edge ideas and thoughts from Edgers around the world.